The Elijah Message

By

Ron and Connie Dahlke

The Elijah Message

Copyright, 2010

Ron Dahlke

Ron.Dahlke@charter.net

Walla Walla, WA 99362

ISBN 978-0-557-88180-2

Preface

Our quest for Bible truth has been a long one – a path that has taken us over many mountains. Sometimes our experience has seemed cohesive, at other times fragmented. For many years we focused mainly on the New Testament, feeling that the "Old Testament" did not pertain.

More recently, to our surprise, we have discovered that the God of the Old Testament is also the God of the New Testament! How does one put this together?

Then there is Malachi 4:4-5, "Remember the Law of Moses My servant, which I commanded him in Horeb for all Israel, with the statutes and judgments. Behold, I will send you Elijah the prophet before the coming of the great and dreadful day of the Lord."

This message of Elijah is clearly an end-time message, for it is to be proclaimed just before "the coming of the great and dreadful day of the Lord." It is also a message of restoration – something has been set aside and is to be restored.

As we set out on a quest to discover this message, we have found that others have intentionally put up stumbling blocks to the reception of this message. Scriptures in the New Testament have been rendered so as to block the validity of the

The Elijah Message

message. The origins and role of Jesus have been "remodeled" to hide the meaning of the message.

But others are also on the same path upon which we have found ourselves. They understand the message and encourage each other. While the message has at times seemed to be muffled to a whisper, in the end it will become the Loud Cry.

Join us as we recount our discoveries.

Ron and Connie Dahlke

Italicized, bold and underlined words are generally our emphasis.

Table of Contents

The Elijah Message

Elijah challenges Israel at Mt. Carmel:
"How long halt ye between two
opinions?" (1 Kings 18:21).

What is the Moral Law?

As a five-year old child, sitting in Bible class and preparing to be a candle-boy, Ron studied the children's lessons on the Law of God. The primary focus was the Ten Commandments. As he read through the material, he noticed that the fourth commandment said, "Remember the Sabbath day to keep it holy. Six days shalt thou labor and do all thy work, but the seventh day is the Sabbath of the Lord thy God." (Exodus 20:8-10).

Looking at the calendar, he saw Sunday was the first day of the week, and Saturday was the seventh day of the week. Why, he asked his pastor, do we go to church on Sunday, when the Bible says the Sabbath is the seventh day? The pastor explained that people worship on Sunday to honor Christ's resurrection. Even as a child, that seemed confusing to Ron. Why would people do something opposite of the Ten Commandments and then say they are keeping God's law?

What is the origin of God's law? Was the law in effect before sin? What did Adam and Eve know before they sinned? These are questions that have come to Ron's mind as an adult.

Although the first written record of the law came at Mt. Sinai, we know Abraham understood and was obedient to God's law: "Abraham obeyed My voice and kept My charge, My commandments, My statutes, and My laws." (Genesis 26:5).

The Elijah Message

We find in Noah's day the law was known: "Then the Lord saw that the wickedness of man was great in the earth, and that every intent of the thoughts of his heart was only evil continually." (Genesis 6:5). Wickedness is defined in terms of rebellion against God's law: "Whoever commits sin transgresses the law, for sin is the transgression of the law." (1 John 3:4). But of Noah, God said, "I have seen that you are righteous before Me in this generation." (Gen. 7:1). Noah was "right doing" – he was keeping God's law.

Even Cain knew the instructions of God's law: "If you do well, will you not be accepted? And if you do not do well, sin lies at the door." (Gen. 4:7). Cain's problem was self-will, thinking he could decide better than God. When Abel's offering was accepted and his was not, he became angry at his brother. "You have heard that it was said to those of old, 'You shall not murder,' and whoever murders will be in danger of the judgment. But I say to you that whoever is angry with his brother without a cause shall be in danger of the judgment." (Matthew 5:21-22). Here Jesus explained how Cain was breaking the sixth commandment, and to Cain it was sin.

Here is a clue: "The *principles* of the ten commandments existed before the fall, and were of a character suited to the condition of a holy order of beings. After the fall, the *principles* of those precepts were not changed, but *additional precepts* were given to meet man in his fallen state."[1] (Emphasis supplied).

---

[1] E. G. White, *Spiritual Gifts,* Vol. 3, p. 295, 1864.

And again, "The law of God existed before the creation of man or else Adam could not have sinned. After the transgression of Adam the *principles* of the law were not changed, but were *definitely arranged and expressed* to meet man in his fallen condition."[2] (Emphasis supplied).

If God had instructed Adam and Eve in the *particulars* of the Ten Commandments, He would have had to explain to them about adultery, murder, lying, and worshiping idols. This would have exposed them to a knowledge of evil. Rather, God gave the *principles* of the Ten Commandments.

When Jesus was asked, "What is the greatest commandment of the law," He replied, "The first of all the commandments is: 'Hear, O Israel, the Lord our God, the Lord is one. And you shall love the Lord your God with all your heart, with all your soul, with all your mind, and with all your strength,' This is the first commandment. And the second, like it, is this: 'You shall love your neighbor as yourself.' There is no other commandment greater than these." (Mark 12:29-31). Matthew reports Jesus' concluding statement as: "On these two commandments hang all the Law and the Prophets." (Matthew 22:40).

When Jesus was asked to give the greatest commandment in the Law, He did not turn to Exodus 20. Rather He quoted from Deut. 6:4-5 and Leviticus 19:18. He quoted the two main *principles* of the law. These are the principles that were known by Adam and Eve in Eden before sin. As sinless, holy beings, this is all they needed to

---

[2] E. G. White, *Signs of the Times,* March 14, 1878.

The Elijah Message

know: Love God supremely; and Love your neighbor impartially. They did what God asked, without question. They did the loving thing towards each other. They did not need to know the *particular* warnings against evil, until they sinned. Then they had to be told the *particulars* of the law that would guard them from hurting God, hurting others, and hurting themselves.

The very definition of *Torah* is: the fence of instruction that protects God's friends. God's law should be welcomed as protective. It keeps us within the circle of God's blessing.

"Blessed are the undefiled in the way, who walk in the *Torah* of the Lord! Blessed are those who keep His testimonies, who seek Him with the whole heart! You have commanded us to keep Your precepts diligently. Oh, that my ways were directed to keep Your statutes! ... I will praise You with uprightness of heart, when I learn Your righteous judgments." (Psalm 119:1-5, 7).

"Blessed are those who do His commandments, that they may have the right to the tree of life, and may enter through the gates into the city." (Revelation 22:14).

"God reigns over the nations; God sits on His holy throne." (Psalm 47:8). Here God's throne is connected to the law by which He reigns.

"Clouds and darkness surround Him; Righteous-ness and justice are the foundation of His throne." (Psalm 97:2). How is God's righteousness and justice expressed? Through His holy law. We see

that God's law, the expression of His righteousness and justice, is the foundation of His throne.

God's law is the unfolding of "Love to God" and
"Love to man." Since God's character is love, the
Law is also the portrayal or transcript of God's
character. For me, this has been an astounding
revelation that portrays the God of the Old
Testament as a God of love, just as the God of the
New Testament is a God of love.

Then we read in John 1:18, "No man hath seen
God at any time; the only begotten Son, who is in
the bosom of the Father, He hath declared Him."
This reflects what Jesus said in John 6:46, "Not
that any man hath seen the Father, save He which
is of God, He hath seen the Father."

In the Old Testament, there are various times
when human beings saw God. Notable verses that
proclaim this are: "Then the Lord *appeared* to
Abram." (Genesis 12:7). Regarding Hagar's
experience: "Then she called the name of the Lord
who spoke to her, You-Are-the-God-Who-Sees: for
she said, 'Have I also here *seen Him* who sees
me?" (Genesis 16:13). Also, "So Jacob called the
name of the place *Peniel*: 'For I have *seen God*
face to face, and my life is preserved." (Genesis
32:30). At the burning bush near Mt. Horeb,
"Moses hid his face, for he was afraid to *look upon
God*." (Exodus 3:6).

According to Jesus, as recorded in the Gospel of
John, these "theophanies" cannot be appearances
of God the Father – they therefore must be
appearances of God the Son. This helps identify

The Elijah Message

the "Angel" sent before the Israelites in the wilderness (Exodus 23:20-21). Note that God said, "Obey His voice ... for My name is in Him." It also explains who gave the renewed Covenant to Israel through Moses in Exodus 34: "Then the Lord said to Moses, 'Write these words, for according to the tenor of these words I have made a covenant with you and with Israel.' So he was there with the Lord forty days and forty nights." (Exodus 34:27-28). That Moses saw the presence of the Lord is evident in vs. 29-30, when it says the skin of Moses' face shown so brightly the people could not bear to look upon him.

We find the Lord in Numbers 12 testified: "Not so with My servant Moses; He is faithful in all My house. I speak with him face to face. ... And *he sees the form of the Lord*." (Numbers 12:7-8). Thus the Lord who spoke with Moses at the tabernacle of meeting, is none other than God the Son. This identifies the Lord who spoke the book of Leviticus to Moses (Leviticus 1:1) as the pre-incarnate Christ, God the Son. Here we have proof positive that Jehovah, the Law Giver of the Old Testament is none other than Jesus Christ, the Savior of the New Testament. How amazing!

"If the Israelites had obeyed God's requirements, they would have been practical Christians. They would have been happy; for they would have been keeping God's ways, and not following the inclinations of their own natural hearts. Moses did not leave them to misconstrue the words of the Lord or to misapply His requirements. He wrote all the words of the Lord in a book, that they might

be referred to afterward. In the mount he had
written them as Christ Himself dictated them."[3]

Is law-keeping taught in the New Testament?
Certainly it is! We find texts such as: "If you love
Me, keep My commandments." (John 14:15).
Jesus also said: "If you keep My commandments,
you will abide in My love, just as I have kept My
Father's commandments and abide in His love.
These things I have spoken to you, that My joy
may remain in you, and that your joy may be full."
(John 15:10-11). Here commandment keeping is
associated with love, abiding in Christ, and joy.

Even believers at the end of time will be keeping
God's commandments: "Here is the patience of
the saints, here are those who keep the
commandments of God and the faith of Jesus."
(Revelation 14:12).

"The Lord would have all His sons and daughters
happy, peaceful, and obedient. Through the
exercise of faith the believer comes into
possession of these blessings. Through faith, every
deficiency of character may be supplied, every
defilement cleansed, every fault corrected, every
excellence developed."[4]

---

[3] E. G. White, *Manuscript Releases*, Vol. 1, p. 114.
[4] E. G. White, *The Acts of the Apostles*, p. 564.

Let No Man Judge You

Despite Paul's assertion "The law is holy, and the commandment holy and just and good" (Romans 7:12), and his statement: "Do we then make void the law through faith? Certainly not! On the contrary, we establish the law" (Romans 3:31), there are those who take Paul's words in various places and say "The law was nailed to the cross."

One verse that is said to mean just such a thing is Colossians 2:14, "Having wiped out the hand-writing of requirements that was against us, which was contrary to us. And He has taken it out of the way, having nailed it to the cross."

I noticed the first part of Colossians 2:14 was not a complete sentence – it seemed to be the ending of the previous sentence. To see the context, I read verse 13: "And you, being dead in your *trespasses* and the uncircumcision of your flesh, He has made alive together with Him, having forgiven you all *trespasses*, having wiped out the handwriting of requirements that was against us, which was contrary to us."

I noticed several things from this text. First, Paul is writing to those who are uncircumcised in their flesh. This can mean only one thing: these are not Jews, but rather Gentiles whom Paul is addressing. Prior to their conversion to the Gospel, they were "dead in trespasses;" they were heathen: pagans worshiping pagan gods, not following God's ways.

Secondly, I noticed the topic of verses 13-14 is how God has dealt with their *trespasses.* God has forgiven their *trespasses,* by taking away the "handwriting." Looking up the Greek term, I found this comes from *cheirographonus dogmassen* – the written accusations.

The picture is like an officer writing out a traffic ticket. Such a traffic ticket specifies which law was broken (the *dogmassen* or requirement), and how and where the law was broken (the *cheirographonus* – the accusation). A fine is specified, and a court date is set.

Some people send in the fine without protest. Other people go to court to protest their innocence, but rarely do they end up with anything but the original fine to pay. A few people ignore the ticket, their legal bond, and hope the court system is too busy to notice. But eventually that seemingly minor traffic ticket turns into an arrest warrant, and the person may find himself in jail until the matter is settled – he may even find his driver's license revoked.

In no instance is the law "done away with" to settle the *cheirographonus dogmassen.* The terms of the law must be satisfied. The penalty must be paid.

As sinners who have broken God's law, we have a much more serious charge against us than a traffic ticket. "The wages of sin is death." (Romans 6:23a). But, praise the Lord, "The gift of God is eternal life in Christ Jesus our Lord." (Romans 6:23b). It is the list of our sins, how we have broken God's law, that Jesus bore in His person on the cross. God's holy law was not done away with to ransom sinners from their fate. It is the list of our sins that constitutes the *cheirographonus dogmassen* that testifies "against us," and that Jesus "nailed to the cross."

This explains verse 15: "Having disarmed principalities and powers, He made a public spectacle of them, triumphing over them in it." It is Satan and his cohorts who love to accuse the saints before God. They tempt people to sin, then gleefully bring the record into God's courtroom. "See what your son or daughter has done?" But Jesus steps forward and says, "That list of sins is no longer valid. I paid the debt for those sins on the cross." Jesus has disarmed the ability of Satan to accuse sinners who take Jesus as their Sacrifice. Jesus has ransomed us from Satan's clutches.

Then I read verse 16: "So [therefore] let no man judge you in food or in drink, or regarding a festival or a new moon, or *Sabbaton.*"

The first thing to keep in mind, in this context, is that man is not our judge. Christ is the one who died for us, and He is our judge.

Secondly, keep in mind that Paul is addressing Gentile believers. Colossae was a small town, and there is no historical evidence that there was a Jewish synagogue at Colossae. Paul had never set foot in Colossae – he was addressing the concerns of believers as reported by Epaphras (see Colossians 1:4, 7; 2:1).

Let No Man Judge You

Paul's instructions to the Colossian believers in verse 16 are straightforward: "Do what Christ has instructed in matters of food and drink, the annual feasts, new moons and *Sabbaton.*" Let's keep it simple. In another place Paul taught: "Therefore, whether you eat or drink, or whatever you do, do all to the glory of God." (1 Corinthians 10:31).

Paul elsewhere instructed Gentile believers "For indeed Christ, our Passover, was sacrificed for us. Therefore let us keep the feast." (1 Corinthians 5:7-8). "Imitate me, just as I also imitate Christ. Now I praise you, brethren, that you remember me in all things and keep the traditions just as I delivered them to you." (1 Corinthians 11:1-2). Here the word "traditions" is from the Greek word *"Paradosis"* which is a "specific reference to Jewish traditionary law" according to *Strong's Exhaustive Concordance.* The literal meaning of *paradosis* is "handed down." Surely these are the "traditions" handed down from God to Moses, as recorded in the *Torah.* If they were man-made traditions, they would have been called *patroparadotos* or the "traditions of the fathers" (see 1 Peter 1:18).

Did Paul keep the feasts after his conversion to the Gospel? Certainly he did, as we find in Acts 18:21: "But took leave of them, saying, 'I must by all means keep this coming feast in Jerusalem; but I will return again to you, God willing." Also, "But I will tarry in Ephesus until Pentecost." (1 Corinth. 16:8). "But we sailed away from Philippi after the Days of Unleavened Bread." (Acts 20:6). "He [Paul] was hurrying to be at Jerusalem, if possible, on the Day of Pentecost." (Acts 20:16).

The Elijah Message

There is interesting commentary on Acts 20 in *The Acts of the Apostles*. The setting is Paul's preaching the "new doctrine by which Jews were released from the observance of the rites of the ceremonial law." This "was regarded by his enemies as daring blasphemy, and they determined that his voice should be silenced."[5]

Instead of boarding the ship that would take him east to the coast of Palestine, Paul headed north and ended up in Philippi. *On the same page,* we are told, "At Philippi Paul tarried to keep the Passover."[6] Then the explanation continues on the next page, "The Philippians were the most loving and truehearted of the apostle's converts, and during the eight days of the feast he enjoyed peaceful and happy communion with them."[7]

It is clear Paul was teaching that even the Jews were released from the rites of the ceremonial law. And then Paul kept Passover with his Gentile converts at Philippi. From this testimony, we can understand Paul did not view the keeping of a Messianic Passover as being part of the rites of the ceremonial law.

Some see such a firm attachment between the animal sacrifices and the days upon which the sacrifices were offered, that they say the two cannot be separated. Yet this is not the picture the Bible presents.

---

[5] E. G. White, *The Acts of the Apostles,* pp. 390.
[6] *Ibid.*
[7] *Ibid,* p. 391.

We find good instruction on this topic as we study Numbers 28-29, which is a listing of the animal sacrifices to be offered on various recurring days. There are sacrifices specified for the "daily," for the seventh-day Sabbath, for the New Moons, for Passover, Feast of Weeks, Trumpets, Atonement, and Tabernacles.

Wait a minute! you say, I didn't know there were sacrifices specified for the seventh-day Sabbath! Yes there were, and it specifically says these sacrifices were in addition to the sacrifices that were offered as part of the "daily." If the religious meaning of the day ceased when the sacrifices ceased, then the seventh-day Sabbath is no longer valid. The truth is, when the sacrifices ceased the religious calendar did not cease. The weekly Sabbath remains, as do the annual festival days. God's religious calendar remains intact.

In fact, we find the weekly seventh-day Sabbath as well as the annual feasts continued to be celebrated by the apostles and by their converts, both Jewish and Gentile, to the close of the New Testament.

What does the reference to the new moons mean (Col. 2:16)? The new moons define the lunar calendar - the calendar that regulates the annual Feasts of the Lord (Passover, Pentecost, Tabernacles, etc.).

We find another reference to New Moons in Isaiah 66:22-23, "'For as the new heavens and the new earth which I will make shall remain before Me,' says the Lord, 'So shall your descendants and your

The Elijah Message

name remain. And it shall come to pass that from one New Moon to another, and from one Sabbath to another, all flesh shall come to worship before Me,' says the Lord." Here we see the New Moons will regulate some aspect of <u>when</u> the redeemed come to worship before God in the New Earth.

What about *Sabbaton* in Colossians 2:16? This is the same word used in Mark 2:27-28, "And He said to them, 'The *Sabbaton* was made for man, and not man for the *Sabbaton*. Therefore the Son of Man is also Lord of the *Sabbaton*." All New Testament references to the seventh-day Sabbath, before and after the cross, come from the Greek word *Sabbaton.* This word is defined by *Strong's* at <u>www.blueletterbible.org</u> as "the seventh day of the week, the Sabbath." This is none other than the weekly seventh-day Sabbath. The word *Sabbaton* is never used in the New Testament to refer to any of the annual feasts, which are referred to in the Greek as *heorte* ("feast; holy day") or *heortazo* ("keep the feast"), or by their given names such as *Pascha* (Passover), *Pentecost*, or *Skenopegia* (Tabernacles).

In Colossians 2:16 Paul is giving a list of things the Gentile believers are not to feel ashamed to practice. Their pagan neighbors were not to be their judges in matters of food and drink, the annual festivals as determined by the lunar calendar, nor the keeping of the weekly seventh-day Sabbath. This is what Paul consistently taught and practiced with his Gentile converts.

Paul goes on in verse 17 to say "why" these things remain important to believers: "Which *are*

14

shadows of things to come, but the substance is of Christ." In the original, this verse could be translated, "Which *are* shadows of things to come, even the substance Christ." The word translated "are" is the Greek word *esti* which means "are" in the present perfect tense. Paul is clear that these good things he is recommending to the Colossians will serve to remind them of good things yet to come, even the substance [*soma:* sound body] Christ. As they eat and drink, they are to do so in reference to Christ and His teachings, including the dietary laws of Torah. As they "keep the feasts" according to the lunar calendar they are to do so in reference to Christ and His plan of salvation – these are yearly reminders of Christ's great provisions for their redemption, even for those who were once dead in trespasses and sins: Christ has brought new life to them. As they observe the seventh-day Sabbath from week to week, they are to do so in reference to Christ, who has provided salvation rest in the present and has promised eternal salvation rest for the future.

God's law is not "against us." Even the Torah, the Book of the Law is not "against us." Turning to Deuteronomy 31:26 and looking up the Hebrew, I found that the phrase "against you" has no Hebrew antecedent in Deuteronomy 31:26. Therefore, when Paul referred to Jesus Christ taking something out of the way that is "against us" he could not have been referring to the Book of the Law in Deuteronomy 31:26, because the phrase "against you" was not in the Hebrew Torah that Paul memorized and loved.

The Elijah Message

"If God be for us, who can be against us!" (Romans 8:31). Our adversary is Satan, not God or His holy law. Jesus Christ was victorious over Satan during His life and on the cross. Satan is a defeated foe. Through Christ's sacrifice He obtained eternal salvation for those who will believe on Him. Through His blood He has obtained justification sufficient for every sinner. Through the power of the Holy Spirit, He has supplied sanctification – a change in our characters to reflect His likeness. Through both justification and sanctification we are set in right relationship to God's holy law and are prepared to live in God's kingdom, not as rebels, but as loving and faithful sons and daughters.

The Jerusalem Council

The Jerusalem Council (held c. AD 48) has been seen as a watershed event for the Christian church.

The background is that around AD 35-36 Peter had been sent to Cornelius, the Roman centurion, to preach the Gospel. Cornelius and his entire household were converted. It was around this time (c. AD 38) that Paul spent 15 days with Peter at Jerusalem (Galatians 1:18).

Paul and Barnabas were ordained as missionaries to the Gentiles, and prior to AD 48 had completed one missionary journey that took them through the southern part of what is now Turkey in Asia Minor.

Working at Antioch, Peter and Paul met again after some years. At first, Peter seemed comfortable associating with Gentile converts, until a delegation arrived from Jerusalem. These were believing Jews, but still enmeshed in the old concept that Jews could not associate with Gentiles. Paul confronted Peter when, under the influence of this Jewish contingent, he turned against his heaven-commanded acceptance of the Gentile believers, and Peter was chastised to return to the path Jesus Christ had pointed out to him years before.

The Elijah Message

Then even more serious trouble arose in Antioch, as the Jewish contingent from Jerusalem realized the Gentiles were being admitted into fellowship without first being circumcised. As the controversy escalated, it was decided an appeal needed to be made for a decision by leaders of the church at Jerusalem. With much prayer, Peter, Paul, Barnabas and others set out to seek counsel.

We must understand that the view of orthodox Judaism at the time held that no Gentile had any hope of salvation. Yes, "God fearing" Gentiles could "convert" and associate with Jews at the synagogue, but in the orthodox Jewish view, they could not hope for everlasting salvation in God's kingdom of Paradise. The Jewish custom was to require various things of the "God fearing" Gentiles prior to being allowed to attend synagogue services. Circumcision was part and parcel of these requirements.

We find the conflict over circumcision and the proceedings of the Jerusalem Council recorded in Acts 15. Peter was the one who presented the clinching argument, that God had accepted the uncircumcised Cornelius and had poured out the Holy Spirit upon him and his household, just as the Holy Spirit had descended upon the circumcised disciples on the Day of Pentecost.

Then James, who appears to have been the one who chaired the meeting, gave his conclusion: "Therefore I judge that we should not trouble those from among the Gentiles who are turning to God, but that we write to them to abstain from things polluted by idols, from sexual immorality, from things strangled, and from blood. For Moses [this is positive] has had throughout many generations those who preach him in every city, being read in the synagogues every Sabbath." (Acts 15:19-21).

As we analyze this statement, several things become clear. The things now prohibited to the Gentiles are basic moral issues that are spelled out in the Law of Moses. This cannot be seen as an unmitigated throwing overboard of the Book of the Law. Meat offered to idols is not specifically mentioned in the Ten Commandments, nor is the general term immorality (fornication), nor the prohibition against things strangled and containing blood. This shows that the teachings in the Law of Moses attach to the various Ten Commandments. Offering meat to idols is against the first commandment: "Thou shalt have no other gods before Me." (Ex. 20:3). Sexual fornication is attached to (but not specifically mentioned by) the seventh commandment. (Ex. 20:14). Surely the eating of strangled meat, filled with blood, (Lev. 3:17; 7:26) is against the sixth commandment: "Thou shalt not kill," (Ex. 20:13) for God said, "The life of the flesh is in the blood." (Lev 17:11; Deut. 12:23). As someone has said, the Ten Commandments are the "headlines," and the statutes and judgments are the "fine print." Each of these four requirements is from the "fine print" in the Law of Moses. Thus, the Jerusalem Council was not "throwing overboard" the Law of Moses, or the *Torah*.

So what <u>were</u> they doing? They were establishing Fellowship Requirements. To attend synagogue services, those Gentiles who were interested in becoming God Fearers were asked to abstain from four things. At the synagogue they would hear *Torah* preached from week to week, as had been done for generations.

As Paul later preached, even the "Jews were released from the rites of the ceremonial law."[8] But not everything in the Book of the Law was the ceremonial law.

"In the book of Leviticus are found many of the special <u>moral</u> requirements which were given to Moses to give to the children of Israel. These were carefully <u>written in a book</u>, and were nothing less than the principles of the Ten Commandments, defining the duty of man to his fellowman, and his obligation to God. ... In doing His commandments was their only happiness and safety."[9]

The Book of the Law contained both Moral Law items and Ceremonial Law items. How can we tell the difference? "In the middle of the week, He [the Messiah] shall bring an end to sacrifices and oblations." (Daniel 9:27). The "oblations" referred to were the grain, wine and oil offerings that were consumed on the altar along with the fat of the sacrifice.

Only the animal sacrificial system ended at the cross. This included the sacrifices themselves, the role of the earthly priests in offering the sacrifices, and the earthly temple as the place to offer sacrifices.

---

[8] E. G. White, *The Acts of the Apostles,* p. 390, 1911.
[9] E. G. White, *The Signs of the Times,* July 22, 1880.

The earthly types ended only as they met their "better" (heavenly) antitypes. Note that the types and the antitypes are "matched pairs." Paul's teaching in Hebrews 7-10 is clear as to the types and the antitypes, and shows what, how and why the ceremonial law ended at the cross. We now have a "better" Sacrifice, a "better" High Priest and a "better" sanctuary to which we look for salvation.

Jesus opened up His religion to be available world-wide, no longer to be centered at Jerusalem. Speaking to the woman at the well of Sychar, He said, "Woman, believe Me, the hour is coming when you will neither on this mountain, nor in Jerusalem, worship the Father. ... But the hour is coming, and now is, when the true worshipers will worship the Father in spirit and truth; for the Father is seeking such to worship Him." (John 4:21, 23). Also, in John 6 we see Jesus focusing on the theme of Passover, at the time of Passover, but He remained at Capernaum during Passover (compare John 6:4 with John 6:59). Jesus disconnected the keeping of the feast with going to Jerusalem, yet He preserved His religious calendar.

Notice that the annual feasts did not come up for discussion at the Jerusalem Council. In fact, we are told the trip to Jerusalem was timed so that the contingent from Antioch would "meet delegates from the different churches and those who had come to Jerusalem to <u>attend the approaching festivals</u>."[10]

---

[10] E. G. White, *The Acts of the Apostles,* p. 190.

The Elijah Message

Those who would teach that these "four things" of Acts 15 comprise *all* the required practice set forth upon the Gentile believers, need to contemplate the following questions:

Why was the seventh-day Sabbath not enjoined upon the Gentiles by the Jerusalem Council?

Why was not tithing specified as an expected practice?

Why is there no specification regarding clean and unclean meats?

It becomes self-evident that these "four things" are merely "beginning steps" – the Fellowship Requirements that were customary for those who would attend synagogue services. "No greater burden" than these four things would be laid upon those who were beginning to learn of the One True God, and wanted to attend synagogue services. Then, during their attendance at synagogue, they would hear "Moses" (the written *Torah*), as it was read from week to week.

Notice also the "final letter" says nothing about circumcision, the original point of contention. It is, however, clear that among the Christian congregations in Paul's day there developed a group called "the Circumcision" and another group called "the Uncircumcision." Paul taught that no one was to be discriminated against because of being circumcised or not being circumcised. Paul held to the teaching of Moses: "Therefore circumcise the foreskin of your heart, and be stiff-necked no longer." (Deut. 10:16). "For he is not a Jew who is

22

one outwardly, nor is circumcision that which is outward in the flesh; but <u>he is a Jew who is one inwardly</u> [this is positive]; and circumcision is that of the heart, in the Spirit, not in the letter; whose <u>praise</u> is not from men but from God." (Rom. 2:28-29).

Two things must be noted: In Acts 16:3 it was Paul who had Timothy circumcised. This was *after* the Jerusalem Council. Also notable were the *false* reports circulated about Paul that he was teaching Jews in the *Diaspora* "to forsake Moses, saying that they ought not to circumcise their children nor to walk according to the customs." (Acts 21:21). Paul's own witness at the end was, "I have done nothing against our people or the customs of our fathers." (Acts 28:17).

Paul taught that Jew and Gentile were to be joined together in "one new man." (Ephesians 2:15). The question becomes: What is this "new man" to look like? What is this "new man" to practice? Are pagan ways and days now admitted into the Christian church? While it can be difficult to read the mind of Paul, he clearly did not envision a divided church, split into factions with widely divergent practices. Paul's teaching in Romans 11 shows that the Gentile converts were to be "grafted in" among the Jewish "remnant," become followers of the True Jew, Jesus Christ, and practice those things specified in the *Torah* that were not part of the animal sacrificial system.

The best way to understand what a teaching means is to find out the practical application of the teaching. How did the decision of the Jerusalem

The Elijah Message

Council play out in the lives of the Gentile Christians? What did Paul teach to his Gentile converts?

Paul honored the decision of the Jerusalem Council. He did not lay circumcision or the ceremonial law upon his Gentile converts. We understand circumcision. Do we understand the ceremonial law?

God gave two types of law: the moral law and the ceremonial law: "God's people, whom he calls his peculiar treasure, were privileged with a two-fold system of law; the moral and the ceremonial."[11] All of God's requirements fit into one or the other. Ellen White says that the moral law was in existence at creation, and the ceremonial law "consisted in sacrifices and offerings pointing to the future redemption."[12]

"The ceremonial law of sacrificial offerings, pointing to Christ, ceased at the death of Christ."[13] "When type met antitype in the death of Christ, the sacrificial offerings ceased. The ceremonial law was done away."[14] "It was only the ceremonial law which was abrogated at the death of Christ."[15] Ellen White informs us that the ceremonial law consisted of the animal sacrifices that pointed to Christ's death. At the cross, only the ceremonial law ended, for the sacrifices no longer had any

---

[11] E. G. White, *The Review and Herald*, "The Law of God," May 6, 1875,

[12] *Ibid.*

[13] E. G. White, *The Signs of the Times*, March 7, 1878.

[14] E. G. White, *The Review and Herald*, June 26, 1900.

[15] E. G. White, *Selected Messages*, Bk. 1, p. 239.

24

role. The sacrifices were only placeholders, to remind the people of the True Sacrifice to come. Now we look to Christ, the True Sacrifice for atonement for our sins.

By studying Hebrews 7-10, we find three things were types that have been overshadowed by their more glorious antitypes. All three "types" were part of the animal sacrificial system:

The animal sacrifices have been overshadowed by Christ's more glorious sacrifice.

The work of the priests who "made atonement for the people" has been overshadowed by the atoning work of Christ, who alone could effect true at-one-ment between man and God.

The role of the earthly sanctuary as the place where atonement "happened," has been overshadowed by the true heavenly sanctuary as the place where atonement happens.

Notice that the types/antitypes are "matched pairs." Only a better Sacrifice could end the animal sacrificial system. Only a better High Priest could bring the atoning work of the earthly priests to an end. Only a more glorious heavenly sanctuary could end the atoning role of the earthly sanctuary.

Getting back to the teaching and practice of Paul, we find that as late as the end of his third missionary journey (c. 58 AD), he was still using the religious calendar of *Torah*. Let's review the sequence of events toward the end of that third missionary journey: Paul was teaching "the new doctrine by which Jews were released from the observance of the rites of the ceremonial law."[16] Paul was a Jew. Did he practice what he taught? If the Jews were released from "the rites of the ceremonial law," wouldn't that have included Paul himself?

Next, we find the reference to the religious calendar Paul followed: "[Paul's] plan to reach Jerusalem in time for the Passover services had to be given up, but he hoped to be there at Pentecost."[17] Some would say, "Well, he was going to Jerusalem to convert the Jews." The very next thing Paul does controverts that idea.

"At Philippi Paul tarried to keep the Passover."[18] Here it cannot be said that Paul was trying to convert the Jews by keeping Passover, for there were hardly any Jews in Philippi - the Christians at Philippi were primarily Gentile converts. But some still say, "Well, it doesn't say the Gentiles kept the Passover." Doesn't it? "The Philippians were the most loving and truehearted of the apostle's converts, and during the eight days of the feast he enjoyed peaceful and happy communion <u>with them</u>."[19]

In the book Paul wrote to the Philippians from Rome, we find this admonition: "The things which you learned and received and heard and saw in me, these do, and the God of peace will be with you." (Philippians 4:9). What was the last thing

---

[16] E. G. White, *The Acts of the Apostles*, p. 390.
[17] *Ibid.*
[18] *Ibid.*
[19] *Ibid.* p. 391.

the Philippian believers saw Paul do? They saw him keeping the Passover! Among other things, they were to keep a Messianic Passover, just as Paul had done with them.

Paul told the same thing to the Corinthians: "For indeed Christ, our Passover, was sacrificed for us. Therefore let us keep the feast." (1 Corinthians 5:7-8). What feast was Paul speaking of? The Passover! Not a Passover where an animal was sacrificed, but a Messianic Passover, the Lord's Supper as recorded in the Gospels.

From eternity, God has had *moed* [set times or appointed times] for His created beings to gather and fellowship with Him. (See Genesis 1:14, Isaiah 14:13). Putting all this together, it seems pretty clear that Christ's religious calendar was not part of the ceremonial law. The apostles continued to honor Christ's religious calendar after Christ's resurrection. It is also clear that Paul continued to teach Christ's religious calendar to his Gentile converts long after the Jerusalem Council.

The Everlasting Covenant

While the Scriptures clearly state, "My covenant I will not break, nor alter the word that has gone out of My lips," (Psalm 89:34), so often people try to put God in a posture of changing this or that. Too many think the "Old Covenant" was the "Book of the Law" and the New Covenant is the Gospel without the Law. They think God was angry in the Old Testament, and became loving and merciful in the New Testament.

Throughout the Old Testament God proclaims the "Everlasting Covenant." Somehow, such a Covenant seems to be unknown today, at least we don't hear it preached by New Testament Christians. Again, this represents the mind-set that the New Testament has no relationship to the Old Testament. But is this what Scripture teaches?

In Genesis 9 is recorded an "Everlasting Covenant" that God made with all living flesh, "The rainbow shall be in the cloud, and I will look on it to remember the everlasting covenant between God and every living creature of all flesh that is on the earth." (Genesis 9:16). Verse 15 explains: "The waters shall never again become a flood to destroy all flesh." Never again would there be a world-wide flood that would wipe all living flesh off the face of the earth.

Did God mean what He said? Has He changed His mind in the last 4,500 years? Every time we see a

The Everlasting Covenant

rainbow, we are assured that this "Everlasting Covenant" that God proclaimed to Noah still stands.

The first promise God made to Adam and Eve after they sinned was when He told the serpent (Satan): "I will put enmity between you and the woman, and between your seed and her Seed; He shall bruise your head and you shall bruise His heel." (Genesis 3:15). A Deliverer was to come, the second Adam, who would reverse the curse and defeat the devil. This was the first Messianic promise, and the shed blood of animals that gave their lives so Adam and Eve might have coverings for their bodies graphically portrayed the horrifying results of sin.

Ellen White's view of the Everlasting Covenant is found in her chapter, "The Law and the Covenants:"[20] 1) it was first given to Adam and renewed to Abraham; 2) it involved faith in the Redeemer to come; 3) it offered pardon and mercy for the penitent; 4) it supplied power for obedience; 5) it is the same as the New Covenant.

The characteristics of the Old Covenant are also described. Under the Old Covenant the people 1) thought they could keep God's law in their own strength; 2) entered into covenant based on their own promises to obey; 3) knew that failure and disobedience meant certain eternal death; 4) did not understand their need of a Savior. Now did God make such a covenant? No! The Israelites made this covenant with God, in their own power.

---

[20] E. G. White, *Patriarchs and Prophets,* pp. 370-372, 1890.

The Elijah Message

Within 40 days of making these promises they were bowing down before the golden calf. The Old Covenant was a dismal failure. It is the disobedient who are under the Old Covenant, for the Old Covenant does not contain God's promises, God's mercy or God's power to obey.

The children of Israel at Sinai finally realized that keeping God's holy law was impossible in their own strength. "They could not hope for the favor of God through a covenant which they had broken; and now, seeing their sinfulness and their need of pardon, they were brought to feel their need of the Saviour revealed in the Abrahamic Covenant and shadowed forth in the sacrificial offerings. Now by faith and love they were bound to God as their deliverer from the bondage of sin. Now they were prepared to appreciate the blessings of the New Covenant."[21]

What comes right after the golden calf incident of Exodus 32-33? In Exodus 34 we find God speaking: "Behold, I make a covenant." (Exodus 34:10). After God proclaims His mercy and justice (Ex. 34:6-7), He speaks the terms of the New/Everlasting Covenant (Ex 34:10-26). "Then the Lord said to Moses, 'Write these words, for according to the tenor of these words *I have made a covenant* with you and with Israel." (Ex. 34:27).

The difference between the New and Old Covenant is simple and clear: The New [Everlasting] Covenant was made by God on behalf of humanity. The Old Covenant is entered into by

---

man trying to impress God – those who would
think they can keep God's law in their own power,
thereby impressing God with their righteousness.
They don't think they need a Savior. Every
apostasy described in Scripture occurred when
people turned their back on the Everlasting
covenant and reverted to the Old Covenant,
setting up their own ways of worship and trying to
recommend themselves to God.

God's law remains the same, and the Covenant He
made has never changed. The question is, which
Covenant do we enter into? Do we accept God's
grace as we bow in repentance before Christ,
accepting His atoning provision on our behalf and
receiving His forgiveness and power to come into
right relationship (obedience) to His law? Or do we
try to keep God's law in our own power, refusing
to recognize our need of Christ and His pardon and
power? We have the choice today to be under the
Old or the New Covenant. However, the Old
covenant has no power and always leads to
disaster, to failure and disobedience. Only the New
Covenant offers a Savior and the power to obey
God's holy law.

That the New Covenant contains God's law is clear
in Jeremiah 31:31-33: "Behold, the days are
coming, says the Lord, when I will make a New
[renewed] Covenant with the house of Israel and
with the house of Judah. ... This is the covenant
that I will make with the house of Israel after
those days, says the Lord: I will put My law in
their minds, and write it on their hearts; and I will
be their God, and they shall be My people."

The Elijah Message

The setting is one of apostasy – Israel had incorporated pagan worship into their practices although they continued to claim they were the "people of God." They had fallen into the Old Covenant. Because of their apostasy, the nation was doomed to be taken into captivity. God allowed them to reap the results of what they sowed. Only when they realized their utter inability to please God in their own strength would they once again be interested in the New Covenant.

Another New Covenant passage is found in Ezekiel 36: "Then I will sprinkle clean water on you, and you shall be clean; I will cleanse you from all your filthiness and from all your idols. I will give you a new heart and put a new spirit within you; I will take the heart of stone out of your flesh and give you a heart of flesh. I will put My Spirit within you and cause you to walk in My statutes, and you will keep My judgments and do them." (Ezekiel 36:25-27). Here we see the New Covenant includes God's law written in the heart, including the statutes and judgments. It's starting to sound a lot like the Elijah message!

At Christ's last Passover supper with His disciples, He proclaimed the New Covenant. Paul was shown this scene in vision, and he reported, "In the same manner He also took the cup after supper, saying, 'This cup is the New Covenant in My blood. This do, as often as you drink it, in remembrance of Me.' For as often as you eat this bread and drink this cup, you proclaim the Lord's death till He comes." (1 Corinthians 11:25-26). To what "New Covenant" was Christ referring? "The covenant of grace was first made with man in Eden [after the

32

fall]. ... Though this covenant was made with Adam and renewed to Abraham, it could not be ratified until the death of Christ. ... When ratified by Christ, it is called a New Covenant. The law of God was the basis of this covenant, which was simply an arrangement for bringing men again into harmony with the divine will, placing them where they could obey God's law."[22] "The Abrahamic covenant was ratified by the blood of Christ, and it is called the 'second,' or 'new,' covenant, because the blood by which it was sealed was shed after the blood of the first [old] covenant [see Exodus 24:5-8]."[23]

It was this New Covenant, determined before the foundation of the world, and spelled out in Exodus 34, that had not been ratified by blood. Christ used the "Cup after Supper" (Luke 22:20) to symbolize His blood that was about to be shed to ratify this New or Everlasting Covenant.

To understand what the "cup after supper" refers to, we do well to understand the elements of the Passover Seder. In the First Century AD/CE the Passover Seder had reached a fairly standard form, including the following elements:

The First Cup – the Cup of Sanctification
The Second Cup – the Cup of Deliverance

The holiday meal

The Third Cup – the Cup of Redemption
The Fourth Cup – the Cup the Kingdom

---

[22] E. G. White, *Patriarchs and Prophets,* pp. 370, 371.
[23] Ibid., p. 371.

The Elijah Message

The singing of the Hallel

The four cups were based on the four "I will" promises that God made in Exodus 6:6-7. The eating of the Passover lamb with unleavened bread and bitter herbs was specified in Exodus 12:8. Eventually, other traditions such as the Four Questions, the breaking and wrapping of the *Afikomen*, and the Cup for Elijah were also incorporated into the Passover *Seder*.

In Luke 22, Jesus used the traditional Passover *Seder* as the basic framework for the Lord's Supper that He instituted. As we work our way through Luke 22 and the other Gospels, we find Christ's Passover was held at the appointed time – just after sundown at the end of Nisan 14 (Luke 22:7, 14); at least two of the "cups" of the *Seder* are mentioned, one being "the cup after supper" (Luke 22:17-18, 20); there was a holiday meal, during which unleavened bread was dipped into sauce (very likely the sauce of bitter herbs) (John 13:26); the disciples are recorded as having asked four questions (John 13:36; 14:5, 8, 22). Jesus' answers to these questions comprise some of the most precious instruction for us contained in the Gospels. Then they sang a *humneo* and went out. [Mark 14:26]. The Greek meaning of *humneo* is "song of praise." This is equivalent to the Hebrew *Hallel* or "psalm of praise." Thus the last item on the agenda before leaving the Upper Room was Jesus and the disciples singing the Passover *Hallel*. (See *The Desire of Ages*, p. 672).

While Jesus participated in the innovations of His day (reclining to show relaxing in freedom); He also added elements such as foot-washing to the Passover *Seder*. The wrapping and hiding away of the broken *Afikomen* was added to Jewish practice during the First Century, and could very well reflect the influence of believers as they practiced the Lord's Supper within the Judeo-Christian context.

"<u>As</u> He ate the Passover with His disciples, He instituted in its place the service that was to be the memorial of His great sacrifice."[24] What is striking about Christ's Lord's Supper is that it was essentially a Passover *Seder* into which He infused Messianic meaning. "[Christ] had just identified Himself with the paschal lamb as its great antitype, by *connecting* the Lord's supper with the Passover."[25] (Emphasis supplied)

Missing from the Lord's Supper was one traditional feature: the roasted lamb. "He Himself was the true paschal lamb, and on the day the Passover was eaten He was to be sacrificed."[26] What day was the Passover commanded to be eaten? At the beginning of Nisan 15 (after sundown that closed out Nisan 14). Thus we see that Friday of Christ's Passion Week was Nisan 15, the first day of Passover. As we study the Gospel accounts, we find Jesus followed the instructions regarding the timing of the Passover meal that He Himself had given to Moses in Exodus 12. Thursday was clearly Nisan 14 (Luke 22:7); Friday was Nisan 15, the

---

[24] E. G. White, *The Desire of Ages*, p. 652.
[25] E. G. White, *The Spirit of Prophecy*, Vol. 3, p. 128.
[26] E. G. White, *The Desire of Ages*, p. 642, 1898

The Elijah Message

first day of Passover; Sabbath was Nisan 16, the second day of Passover; Sunday was Nisan 17, the third day of Passover.

We also see that the Sadducees who controlled the temple services followed their own schedule for the Passover. While the traditional directions called for visual observation of the new moon crescent to begin the months, the Sadducees had devised a calendar based on astronomical observations and mathematical calculations. With this method they could predict the timing of the feasts and set a calendar in advance. Unfortunately, sometimes they were "off" by a day or more from the calendar that was based on the visual observation of the new moon crescent.

The Sadducees also had "offsets" for their calendar: man-made rules that were used to alter the law as given to Moses. An example of an offset was the rule that Passover could never be on the day prior to, nor on the day following the weekly seventh-day Sabbath: Passover could never be on the sixth nor on the first day of the week. While we do not know if the discrepancy between Christ's calendar and the Sadducee's calendar was due to the visual observation of the new moon crescent, or because of the "offset" rule, we can tell by the Gospels that there was a discrepancy. So we must ask: "Who is our example?" Do we follow Jesus Christ or the Sadducees?

The saying "on the third day" was one of Christ's strongest teachings as He approached His crucifixion. He thereby revealed the "time-clock" prophesied in Scripture: "After two days He will revive; on the third day He will raise up." (Hosea 6:2). Jesus clearly connected His resurrection with the waving of the Early Firstfruits (barley sheaf), by the saying, "Unless a kernel of grain [Gk: *situ* – unspecified grain] falls into the ground and dies, it abideth alone; but if it dies, it bringeth forth much fruit." (John 12:24). Paul also taught, "But now Christ is risen from the dead, and has become the firstfruits of those who have fallen asleep. ... But each one in his own order: Christ the firstfruits, afterward those who are Christ's at His coming." (1 Corinthians 15:20, 23).

Jesus knew, according to Hosea 6:2, that the year the Waving of the Early Firstfruits (*Yom HaBikkurim*) fell on the third day of Passover, was the year He would be crucified. This was God's time-clock of prophecy. That year, the day after *Sabbaton* was both the third day of Passover (Nisan 17) and also the day for the waving of the barley sheaf, the Day of Early Firstfruits. Ellen White testified that she saw, "A halo of light and glory clustered about the time of Jesus' death and resurrection, *immortalizing* the sacred facts that He was the Saviour of the world."[27] When did Jesus die? On Nisan 15. When did Jesus rise from the tomb? On Nisan 17, the third day of Passover. This shows that Jesus "reset" the *omer.* The counting of the omer, the 50-day count toward *Shavuot/* Pentecost, should now begin on the third day of Passover, on Nisan 17, for the third day of Passover has been eternally memorialized as the day of Early Firstfruits .

---

[27] E. G. White, *Spiritual Gifts,* Vol. 1, p. 87.

The Elijah Message

Passover reminds us of Christ's sacrifice for our deliverance from the Egypt of sin. Jesus antici-pated Passover into the Kingdom of God when He said, "I will no longer eat of it <u>until</u> it is fulfilled in the kingdom of God." (Luke 22:16).

Because of Christ's sacrifice as the true Passover Lamb, and because of His resurrection as the Firstfruits of those who sleep, we have the assurance that in Christ, we also will be resurrected at Christ's second coming. How important to our faith and our salvation that Christ not only died, but that He also overcame death, rose from the tomb, and now sits at the right hand of the throne of God!

What Christ proclaimed regarding the cup after supper: "This cup is the New Covenant in My blood" (Luke 22:20; 1 Corinth. 11:25), is His teaching that it would be His shed blood that ratified the Everlasting Covenant. Passover portrays the terms of the New Covenant. It shows us our Savior who has redeemed us so that He can offer us mercy, pardon and power.

By His sacrificial death, Jesus procured all the blessings of the New Covenant for us. He is our Savior, offering mercy and pardon, and the power of His grace to live His law from our hearts. Wonderful Savior!

The Gospel and the Rule of Faith

We have seen how Paul regularly kept the feasts, whether at Jerusalem (Acts18:21) or with his Gentile converts in Asia Minor (1 Corinth. 16:8) or Europe (Acts 20:6). We have seen that Paul regularly instructed his Gentile converts to keep the feasts (1 Corinth. 5:7-8; 1 Corinth. 11:1-2; Colossians 2:16). "Feast" language is also embedded in Philippians 4, with the mention of "the Book of Life" (vs. 3); "rejoice in the Lord always" (vs. 4); the mention of the double meaning of *anah* – to be abased and also to abound; and being full before being hungry [*Yom Kipper* talk] (vs. 12).

We know that Jesus kept the feasts, both at Jerusalem (John 2:13; 5:1; 7:10; 10:22-23;12:1) and away from Jerusalem (John 6 – compare verses 4 and 59). Jesus taught that the worship of God was no longer to be centered at Jerusalem (John 4:21-24) – it was now to be opened up and available worldwide.

Never do we see Jesus offering an animal sacrifice during His life on earth. He was the True Sacrifice – He offered up Himself as a ransom for many, that all who believe in Him would not perish but have eternal life. (John 3:16). While "Christ passed through all the experiences of His childhood, youth, and manhood without the observance of ceremonial temple worship,"[28] yet

---

[28] E. G. White, *The Bible Echo*, October 31, 1898.

we do see Him in the temple during the feasts, participating in the activities along with the rest of the throng (John 7:37-38), often reshaping events (John 2:14-19) much to the consternation of the religious leaders. The term "ceremonial worship" like the term "ceremonial law" has to do with the offering of animal sacrifices, and that is something Jesus did not participate in.

"The principles presented by Christ, the manner of observing feasts, of praying to God, could not be properly united to the forms and ceremonies of Phariseeism."[29] What does this say? Christ not only taught His disciples how to pray (Matthew 6:9-15), but He also taught "the manner of observing feasts." We see Him doing this both during Passover (John 6; Luke 22) and during the Feast of Tabernacles (John 7:10-39). Why would He teach the disciples how to observe the feasts if they were to be abolished in a short time?

That Christ did not teach His disciples to abolish the feasts is clear from Acts 2. The Holy Spirit descended "on the very day" of Pentecost (Acts 2:1) – known in Hebrew as *Shavuot* or the Feast of Weeks. A careful study of Acts 2 shows the disciples were in the temple when the Holy Spirit descended upon them. The very word "house" is from the Greek word *oikos*, which means "house" or "temple," and is the same word used in the verse: "And said unto them that sold doves, 'Take these things hence: make not My Father's house [*oikos*] an house [*oikos*] of merchandise." (John 2:16).

---

[29] E. G. White, *The Signs of the Times*, September 19, 1892.

The Gospel and the Rule of Faith

Think of the logistics of the moment. If Peter was preaching from a window or balcony of the Upper Room, and 3,000 of those who heard his preaching were converted and baptized, how could 3000 people fit into the narrow streets of Old Jerusalem?

Rather, the text says that the when the Holy Spirit descended, there was a *loud noise*, and people came running to where Peter was at (Acts 2:2, 6). The disciples were among a crowd of strangers when they began speaking in tongues (Acts 2:7-8), and it was the priests who accused them of being "drunk with new wine." (Acts 2:13).

So we must ask: where were strangers (Jews from the *Diaspora*) gathered to observe *Shavuot/* Pentecost? Where were the priests who mocked and accused the disciples? Where was the "new wine" prepared for the attendees at the feast? All these things were located *at the temple*!

"And when this sound occurred, the multitude came together, and were confounded, because everyone heard them speak in his own language." (Acts 2:6)

"The scene is one full of interest. Behold the people coming from all directions to hear the disciples witness to the truth as it is in Jesus. They press in, *crowding the temple*."[30]

"The Jewish *leaders* had supposed that the work of Christ would end with His death; but, instead of this, *they witnessed* the marvelous scenes of the

---

[30] E. G. White, *The Acts of the Apostles*, p. 42, 1911.

The Elijah Message

Day of Pentecost."[31] "The *priests and rulers* were greatly enraged at this wonderful manifestation, but they dared not give way to their malice, for fear of exposing themselves to the violence of the people. ... The priests, determined to account for the miraculous power of the disciples in some natural way, declared that they were drunken from partaking largely of the new wine *prepared for the feast*."[32]

So we must ask: If the feasts ended at the cross, what is the explanation for Pentecost? The disciples were clearly attending services at the temple on an established feast-day. *Pentecost* means "50 days" and was the term for the feast of *Shavuot* among Greek-speaking Jews for some 200 years before the events recorded in Acts 2.

The theme of *Shavuot* was the giving of the law at Mt. Sinai as part of the Covenant. This was considered to be the event that forged the Israelites into a nation under God. At that time, they became God's "kingdom of priests and a holy nation." (Exodus 19:6). Isn't it interesting that God honored the day of *Shavuot*/Pentecost as the day to anoint His Jewish disciples and all future believers, both Jew and Gentile, as His "chosen generation, a royal priesthood, a holy nation, His own special people, that you may proclaim the praises of Him who called you out of darkness into His marvelous light; who once were not a people but are now the people of God, who had not

---

[31] *Ibid.,* p. 44.
[32] *Ibid.,* p. 40.

obtained mercy but now have obtained mercy." (1 Peter 2:9-10).

Here is what Scripture says:

The Feasts of the Lord were proclaimed to Moses by the pre-incarnate Christ (Leviticus 23 – compare Numbers 12:6-8 and Leviticus 1:1).

The Feasts were observed by Jesus when He walked this earth among His disciples. He even taught the proper way to observe the feasts. There is no evidence that He abolished the feasts, and plenty of evidence that the disciples, both Jew and Gentile observed the feasts after the cross. To the close of the New Testament there is no indication that either the weekly seventh-day Sabbath or the annual feasts were abolished. Rather than being historical occasions only, they became memorials of Christ's acts of salvation on behalf of believers, and were prophetic exercises of the future culmination of salvation events when all the redeemed would gather in person around their Savior at His glorious second coming.

Turning now to historical sources: Are there indications of continued observance of the feasts by the early Christians?

Eusebius was one of the earliest church historians. He gathered various documents, some of which were very old by his time, usually to augment his viewpoint of the history of the church. Eusebius wrote near the beginning of the fourth century AD.

The Elijah Message

One of the viewpoints of Eusebius was that the Bishop of Rome was the rightful leader of the entire Christian church. By the middle of the second century, the Christian world had been divided into three main regions that circled the Mediterranean.

Alexandria, with its fine libraries, became the headquarters that supervised the church in North Africa, including the Coptic Church.

Another region was headquartered at Antioch, long a center of Christian activity. Antioch supervised the Christian churches in Asia Minor and southern Europe in areas such as Greece and Macedonia. This became known as the "Eastern" church.

The Western (European) church was head-quartered at Rome. Because the culture was unique at the capitol of the Roman empire, the issues for the early Christians at Rome were not the same as those faced by the churches in Asia Minor. At Rome, the Christians faced the Emperor (including emperor worship) up close and personal. If things went badly in Rome, the Jewish quarter was often blamed, even when the Jews were innocent. To the pagan Romans, there was no visible difference between the Jews and the Christians. Both groups worshiped on *Shabbat* and both groups kept Passover. Therefore, when the Jews were persecuted, so were the Christians. Little by little, the Christian leaders edged toward practices by which they could distance themselves from the Jewish population. The changes were gradual, but steady. These changes in practice

The Gospel and the Rule of Faith

were not accepted by the Christian churches in Asia Minor.

Eusebius was attached to the Roman church - it was his viewpoint that the Bishop at Rome held highest authority over all the Christian churches. Rome should lead, and all the rest should follow. To prove his point, Eusebius collected documents that showed how stubborn the churches in Asia Minor were in resisting the Bishop of Rome. It is through these documents that we know something of the conflict within the Christian church during the early centuries.

One of the documents Eusebius collected pertained to a Christian leader named Polycarp who was a disciple of John the Revelator. Polycarp was a young man when the apostle John died. Polycarp eventually became the bishop, or leader, of the Christian church at Smyrna in Asia Minor, and as a leader he came into conflict with Anicetus, the Bishop of Rome at the time.

From the *SDA Bible Commentary*, Vol. 9, p. 362 (quotation #655) we find a translation of a letter written by Irenaeus to Victor, Bishop of Rome around 193 AD, regarding the controversy between Polycarp and Anicetus. "When the blessed Polycarp was staying in Rome in the time of Anicetus, though they disagreed a little about some other things as well, they immediately made peace, having no wish for strife between them on this matter [the Easter vs Passover controversy]. For neither was Anicetus [Bishop of Rome] able to persuade Polycarp not to observe it [Passover on Nisan 14], inasmuch as he [Polycarp] had always

45

done so in company with John the disciple of our Lord and the other apostles with whom he had associated; nor did Polycarp persuade Anicetus to observe it [Passover on Nisan 14], for he said that he [Anicetus] ought to keep the custom of those who were presbyters before him [in keeping Easter]."[33] The historical record notes that Polycarp was later arrested (c. 154 AD) and martyred on Passover.

The interesting thing about this historical record is the statement that Polycarp kept Passover "in company with John the disciple of our Lord and the other apostles with whom he had associated." Their Passover was observed at the end of Nisan 14, and followed the example of our Lord during the Lord's Supper. As we have seen, the Lord's supper was a Passover *Seder* infused with Messianic meaning. The elements of the Messianic Passover *Seder* teach about Jesus Christ and His plan of salvation. This letter shows that to the end of the first century the original disciples as well as other apostles who came to leadership, continued to keep the Lord's Supper/Passover yearly at the end of Nisan 14.

The next authenticated quotation (#656) on p. 362 of the *SDA Bible Commentary*, Vol. 9, is a translation of a letter that was written at the end of the second century (after 193 AD) by another Christian leader in Asia Minor, a man by the name of Polycrates who was the bishop or leader of the

---

[33] Eusebius, *Ecclesiastical History*, v. 24, 16, 17, - translated by Kirsopp Lake, Vol 1, Cambridge, Mass, Harvard University Press, 1949, pp. 511, 513).

The Gospel and the Rule of Faith

church at Ephesus. It is said that Polycrates was a disciple of Polycarp (disciple of John the Revelator). Ephesus was John's old pastoral district, and a significant church in Asia Minor. This means Polycrates was a significant leader among the churches in Asia Minor. The letter was written to Victor, the Bishop of Rome at the time:

"Therefore we keep the day [Passover at the end of Nisan 14] undeviatingly, neither adding nor taking away, for in Asia [Minor] great luminaries sleep, and they will rise on the day of the coming of the Lord, when He shall come with glory from heaven and seek out all the saints. Such were Philip ... and two of his daughters. ... There is also John, who lay on the Lord's breast. ... And there is also Polycarp at Smyrna, both bishop and martyr. ... All these kept the fourteenth day of the Passover *according to the gospel*, never swerving, but following *according to the rule of the faith*. And I also, Polycrates, the least of you all, live according to the tradition of my kinsmen, and some of them have I followed. For seven of my family were bishops and I am the eighth, and my kinsmen ever kept the day when the people put away the leaven. Therefore, brethren, I who have lived sixty-five years in the Lord and conversed with brethren from every country, and have studied all holy Scripture, am not afraid of threats, for they have said, who were greater than I, 'It is better to obey God rather than men.' ... And I could mention the bishops who are present whom you required me to summon, and I did so. If I should write their names they would be many multitudes."[34]

---

[34] *Ibid*, pp. 505, 507, 509.

The Elijah Message

It appears that Victor, Bishop of Rome, wrote a threatening letter to Polycrates, bishop at Ephesus, demanding the churches of Asia Minor give up their practice of Passover at the end of Nisan 14 and instead bow to the Bishop of Rome in the matter of Easter. As demanded by the Bishop of Rome, Polycrates had assembled the pastors and leaders of Asia Minor to consider the matter. What were they going to do? They decided to "obey God, rather than man." They listed as their examples none other than John the Revelator, Philip the Evangelist, Polycarp the martyr and other apostles and leaders who had served the Christian church in Asia Minor during the 160 years since Christ's ascension.

Victor, Bishop of Rome, carried through on his threats. He excommunicated the whole lot! Those who would not bow to his demands were not his kind of Christians.

The celebration of Easter as the day of Christ's resurrection became the "gateway holiday" that elevated Sunday as the day of Christian worship. Gradually the seventh-day Sabbath became a minor day to attend prayer at church and then go about one's business; and gradually the sanctity of the Sabbath was transferred to Sunday. This distanced the Christians from the Jews, and it made Christianity more comfortable for the pagans, who had always seen "The Venerable Day of the Sun" as their main day of worship.

Christ commanded the Feasts of the Lord in Leviticus 23. According to the gospel record, Christ kept the feasts and taught their proper

The Gospel and the Rule of Faith

observance. The disciples and the apostles continued to keep the feasts after the cross. Faithful Christians, especially in Asia Minor, continued to keep the feasts to the end of the 2nd century and beyond. It was the Bishop of Rome who took away the Levitical feasts.

"Dear Friend, I have offered and still offer $1000 to any one who can prove to me from the Bible alone that I am bound, under grievous sin to keep Sunday holy. It was the Catholic Church which made the law obliging us to keep Sunday holy. The church made this law long after the Bible was written. Hence said law is not in the Bible. Christ, our Lord empowered His church to make laws binding in conscience. He said to His apostles and their lawful successors in the priesthood 'Whatsoever you shall bind on earth shall be binding in heaven.' Math. 16:19. Math. 18:17. Luke 16:19. The Cath. Church abolished not only the Sabbath, but all the other Jewish festivals. Pray and study. I shall be always glad to help you as long as you honestly seek the truth."[35]

"The new law has its own spirit ... and its own feasts which have taken the place of those appointed in the law of Moses. If we would know the days to be observed ... we must go to the Catholic Church, not to the Mosaic Law."[36]

"As the sign of the authority of the Catholic Church, papist writers cite 'the very act of changing the Sabbath into Sunday, which the Protestants allow of; ... because by keeping Sunday, they acknowledge the church's power to ordain feasts, and to command them under sin.' Henry Tuberville, *An Abridgment of the Christian Doctrine*, p. 58."[37]

The historical record is clear, both from the documents of the early centuries and also from

---

[35] Bishop T. Enright, CSSR, in a letter dated June 1905, St. Alphonsus' Catholic Church, St. Louis, MO.
[36] *The Catholic Catechism,* quoted in *Signs of the Times,* Nov. 4, 1919.
[37] Quoted in *The Great Controversy,* p. 448, 1911.

more modern sources. Christ did not abolish His religious calendar. The faithful Christians in the early church maintained the religious calendar as Christ practiced it.

Not only were Christ's feasts taken away by the Bishop of Rome, but spurious substitutes were put in their place. More than one hundred years after Easter was established as a "Christian" holiday, another pagan festival was brought into the church and given a "Christian" remodel.

"Within the Christian Church no such festival as Christmas was ever heard of till the third century, and that not till the fourth century was far advanced did it gain much observance. How, then, did the Romish Church fix on December the 25th as Christmas-day? Why, thus: Long before the fourth century, and long before the Christian era itself, a festival was celebrated among the heathen, at that precise time of the year, in honour of the birth of the son of the Babylonish queen of heaven; and it may fairly be presumed that, in order to conciliate the heathen, and to swell the number of the nominal adherents of Christianity, the same festival was adopted by the Roman Church, giving it only the name of Christ. ... Upright men strove to stem the tide, but in spite of all their efforts, the apostacy [sic] went on, till the Church, with the exception of a small remnant, was submerged under Pagan superstition. That Christmas was originally a Pagan festival, is beyond all doubt."[38]

---

[38] Alexander Hislop, *The Two Babylons,* "Christmas," p. 93, c. 1855.

"To get the Christian and Pagan festivals amalgamated, and, by a complicated but skilful adjustment of the calendar, it was found no difficult matter, in general, to get Paganism and Christianity – now far sunk in idolatry – in this as in so many other things, to shake hands."[39] The "Babylonish queen of heaven" was Ishtar, also known as Astarte, Venus, Diana etc. Her son Tammuz was born on December 25. Thus we see that the origins of Easter and the December 25 holiday go straight back to Babylonish sun-god worship. Read Jeremiah 7:18 and Ezekiel 8:13-14, 18 to find what God thinks about bringing these practices into the church.

Note the Catholic view: "In observing the Sunday, in keeping Christmas and Easter, they [the Protestants] are accepting the authority of the spokesman for the church, the pope."[40] The only authority for Christians to keep holidays such as Sunday, Easter, Christmas, Lent, Cupid's Day, Halloween and others, is the authority of Rome, the entity that brought them into the Christian church in the first place.

Who is our leader?

What is wrong with Christmas and Easter? 1) They are not taught in Scripture as part of Christ's religion. 2) Both December 25 and Easter Sunday were pagan religious holidays long before the Christian era. They have their roots deep in heathen mythology (fables). 3) Both December 25 and

---

[39] *Ibid.,* "Easter," p. 105.
[40] *Our Sunday Visitor,* February 5, 1950.

The Elijah Message

Easter Sunday are in opposition to what the Bible teaches. Scripture clearly teaches that Jesus was NOT born in the winter (see Luke 2:8). If you are a student of the Word, you will discover clear evidence (from Luke 1:5 comparing 1 Chron. 24:1) that John the Baptist was born near the time of Passover in the spring, and Jesus – being born six months later – was born near the time of the Feast of Tabernacles in the fall. Easter is a little trickier, but the original pagan specification was that the Easter rites were held the first Sunday after the Vernal Equinox. Passover always came later than that – often a month later. The specification of a day (Sunday) rather than the date (Nisan 17) as the marker of Christ's resurrection, flies in the face of the annual Jewish festivals and how they were celebrated. 4) Much of the "cultural trimmings" of Christmas and Easter come straight out of paganism. Can Christ be joined with Belial?

"God will have a people upon the earth to maintain the Bible, and the Bible only, as the standard of all doctrines and the basis of all reforms. ... Before accepting any doctrine or precept, we should demand a plain 'Thus saith the Lord' in its support."[41]

"Between the laws of men and the precepts of Jehovah will come the last great conflict of the controversy between truth and error. Upon this battle we are now entering – a battle not between rival churches contending for the supremacy, but

---

[41] E. G. White, *The Spirit of Prophecy*, Vol. 4, p. 413, 1884.

between the religion of the Bible and the religions of fable and tradition."[42]

"I saw the mercy and goodness of God in sending a warning to the people of the earth, and repeated messages ... that they might divest themselves of errors which have been handed down from the heathen and papists."[43]

"In the commission to His disciples, Christ not only outlined their work, but gave them their message. Teach the people, He said, 'to observe all things whatsoever I have commanded you.' The disciples were to teach what Christ had taught. That which He had spoken, not only in person, but through all the prophets and teachers of the Old Testament, is here included. Human teaching is shut out. There is no place for tradition, for man's theories and conclusions, or for church legislation. No laws ordained by ecclesiastical authority are included in the commission. None of these are Christ's servants to teach. 'The law and the prophets,' with the record of His own words and deeds, are the treasure committed to the disciples to be given to the world. Christ's name is their watchword, their badge of distinction, their bond of union, the authority for their course of action, and the source of their success. **Nothing that does not bear His superscription is to be recognized in His kingdom.**"[44] (Emphasis supplied)

---

[42] E. G. White, *Prophets and Kings,* p. 625, 1917.
[43] E. G. White, *Early Writings,* p. 250, 1858.
[44] E. G. White, *The Desire of Ages,* p. 826, 1898.

The Statutes and Judgments and the Moral Law

We have traced the Moral Law from the throne of God to the Ten Commandments. We have seen that the law and the statutes and judgments are part of the New Covenant. The Elijah message of Malachi 4:4 says "Remember the Law of Moses ... with the statutes and judgments."

The "Law of Moses" is a reference to *Torah*. In fact, if you look up the Hebrew, it really says, "The *Torah* of Moses." This is what was written by Moses in a book, and stored "in the sides [Heb. *tsad* – "side" or "sides"]" (Deut. 31:26) of the Ark of the Covenant. As we have already noted, the original Hebrew does not say this Book of the Law is "against you." The phrase "against you" has no antecedent in the original Hebrew of Deut. 31:26. The text simply states that the Book of the Law would be a "witness." The word translated "witness" means "face." A witness is simply to tell what happened in their presence. A witness is not to shape his testimony to be "for" or "against" the person on trial. A witness is simply to tell what they saw happen. The *Torah* witnesses to us and tells us God's ways.

What are the statutes and judgments, and how do they relate to the Ten Commandments?

The Statutes and Judgments

We know "Abraham obeyed My [God's] voice, and kept My charge, My commandments, My statutes, and My laws." (Genesis 26:5). Unfortunately, we do not know much about the particulars of these commands, statutes and laws that Abraham obeyed.

We know that Noah knew about the clean and unclean animals (Genesis 7:2; 8:20), for only clean animals could be sacrificed to God. But we are not told any particulars.

We know Abraham and Jacob on occasion gave a tithe (Genesis 14:20; 28:22), but this is presented as an unusual practice. To whom did Jacob pay his tithe? Considering that in later years the tithe was taken to the sanctuary and eaten by the worshipers as part of the festivals, perhaps Jacob held a large feast for his family and any interested surrounding neighbors, giving thanks to God, using the promised tithe in this manner.

There are many things the ancients knew and practiced that are not spelled out in the record. The first written codification of God's law came at Mt. Sinai. That is where God proclaimed the Ten Commandments to the people and wrote them on the two tablets of stone. Some would look, therefore, to these two tablets of stone as the sum total of the Moral Law. But Jesus did not teach any such thing. In His sermon on the Mount (Matthew 5-7), and in His answer to the question: Which is the greatest commandment (Mark 12:28-31), Jesus broadened the concept beyond thinking that God's Law is only what was written on the two tablets.

The Elijah Message

There is another difficulty in accepting only the two tablets as the definitive source of God's Law. Has anyone seen these two tablets lately? These two tablets have not been seen since the Ark of the Covenant was secreted by Jeremiah in a cave near Jerusalem just prior to the last conquest of Jerusalem by Nebuchadnezzar in 586 B.C. That was more than 2500 years ago! Without the written *Torah* of Moses that was preserved in the temple complex, we would have no record today of God's law, moral or otherwise.

Some people would say: "Well, Jesus is the embodiment of God's law. I just do what He did." That is a good viewpoint, but those who say this often do not do what Jesus did. They do what they <u>like</u> that Jesus did. And often they misinterpret or discard many principles and practices that Jesus lived and taught. Everything that Jesus did was consistent with the *Torah* that He Himself revealed to Moses.

The essential problem with much of nominal Christianity today is that it has discarded the backdrop that was in place when Jesus lived and taught. Take away the background, change it to a Gentile, pagan mindset, and suddenly Jesus can become anything a person imagines. This, however, does injustice to the Biblical record, and promotes a "false Jesus."

We need to restore the background. We need to understand *Torah*. It was the pre-incarnate Christ who gave these commands, precepts and principles to Moses. The things that ended at the cross are discussed in Hebrews 7-10. We call this the "ceremonial law." Actually, such a term is not found in scripture. Specifically, the "ceremonial law" is comprised of those regulations pertaining directly to the offering of animal sacrifices. These things were "types" that ended when they met their "better" anti-type in Jesus Christ. The types and antitypes were "matched pairs." Nothing ended except that it has been replaced with "something better." Wherever Torah speaks of an animal sacrifice, there we need to lift up Jesus Christ: His sacrifice on the cross, and His atoning work today in the heavenly sanctuary as He pleads His shed blood on our behalf.

"That the obligations of the <u>Decalogue</u> might be more fully understood and enforced, additional precepts were given, illustrating and applying the principles of the <u>Ten Commandments</u>. These laws were called judgments."[45]

The setting is Mount Sinai. God has spoken the Ten Commandments, and the people are afraid – very afraid. They tremble. They plead with Moses that they should not hear God's voice anymore, for it frightens them. God concedes to their wishes, and says He will speak the rest of His require-ments to Moses privately. The result is that the judgments were spoken directly to Moses.

These judgments are found in Exodus 21, 22 and 23. We are told these are a fuller understanding of the Decalogue, they are the principles of the Ten Commandments. Certainly this attaches these judgments to the moral law.

[45] E. G. White, *Patriarchs and Prophets*, p. 310, 1890.

The Elijah Message

What are these judgments?

"The first of these laws related to servants. ... Manstealing, deliberate murder, and rebellion against parental authority were to be punished with death. ... The murderer of a slave was to be punished; an injury inflicted upon one by his master, though no more than the loss of a tooth, entitled him to his freedom."[46] This is an exposition of Exodus 21:1-11.

This sounds like the Moral Law to me! In fact, each of these judgments can be connected back directly to one of the Ten Commandments. The Ten Commandments are the "headlines," and the judgments are the "fine print."

"The rights of widows and orphans were specially guarded, and a tender regard for their helpless condition was enjoined. ... Aliens who united themselves with Israel were to be protected from wrong or oppression [Exodus 22:21-22]."[47]

The support of widows, orphans, the poor and the stranger is part of the Moral Law. These stipulations protecting the vulnerable connect directly back to the admonition, "Thou shalt not covet." (Exodus 20:17). The support of the poor is further delineated in Deut. 12:12, 18-19; 14:27-29; 15:7-11; 26:12-13. Notice how the poor and needy were to share in the tithe of the third year, along with the Levites.

---

[46] *Ibid.*, p. 310.
[47] *Ibid.*, pp. 310-311.

The Statutes and Judgments

While we are on the topic, let us note another thing about the tithe. Some point to Numbers 18:24 and say that all the tithe should go to the "Levites." That is not what the text says. It says the heave offering of the tithe belongs to the Levites. The heave offering was 1/10 of the tithe apportioned to the Levites every third year. It was the portion of the tithe that went to support the central sanctuary services. The Levites were to partake locally of the tithe of every third year, along with the widows, orphans and strangers in need. One-tenth of the tithe that the Levites received, they were to pass along to the central sanctuary. This was the "heave offering." (see also Number 18:19, 25-32; Deut. 14:22-29).

Numbers 18:24 is a clarification of Numbers 18:21, "Behold, I have given the children of Levi all the tithes in Israel as an inheritance." Let us not turn one text against another. The word "all" means that no portion of the specified tithe was to be withheld from the Levites. In other words, the Levitical tithe collected (every third year) in the northern part of Israel was not to be withheld from any Levite in Israel who needed it, regardless of where he lived. The same was true for tithes collected in southern Israel, western Israel, the Jordan valley, and the lands of the tribes east of the Jordan. The tithe was to be collected locally, but shared throughout the land as needed. Levites in one area were not to be partitioned off from receiving the tithe of another area. The needs of all were to be met equitably. Also note that the Levites were to receive from the "storehouse" according to need (Deut. 14:28). There was to be no accumulation of wealth. They were without a

landed inheritance, but the specified tithe was
their inheritance, according to their need.

Another misperception relates to "who were the
Levites?" Some assume that all Levites were
priests, but that is not true. Only the descendants
of Aaron were priests. Yet all non-priest Levites
were religious workers, serving but a portion of
their time at the sanctuary. The remainder of their
time was spent locally, teaching the people the
Law of God and supporting religious activities in
their local area. This shows that local religious
workers today (including teachers in church
schools) are the modern version of the Levites of
Bible times. All these were to be supported by the
tithe of the third year.

Continuing on with the judgments: "The taking of
usury from the poor was forbidden. ... Respect for
magistrates and rulers was enjoined, and judges
were warned against perverting judgment, aiding
a false cause, or receiving bribes."[48] This is
commentary on Ex. 22:25-28. The commandments involved are "Thou shalt not steal," "Thou
shalt not covet," and "Honor thy father and thy
mother." (See Exodus 20:12-17).

"Again the people were reminded of the sacred
obligation of the Sabbath. Yearly feasts were
appointed."[49] These commands relate to the fourth
commandment, the Sabbath commandment.
These commands also relate to "Thou shalt have
no other gods before Me," and "Thou shalt not

[48] Ibid., p. 311.
[49] Ibid., p. 311.
60

bow down to graven images." If followed both in spirit and letter, these commands would have preserved Israel true to the God of Abraham, Isaac and Jacob. These commands shut out pagan practices and pagan holidays. They were not to bring abominations into the camp.

"The object of all these regulations was stated: they proceeded from no exercise of mere arbitrary [capricious] sovereignty; all were given for the good of Israel. The Lord said, 'Ye shall be holy men unto Me' – worthy to be acknowledged by a holy God."[50] Do we need to be "holy men," "worthy to be acknowledge by a holy God?" If so, we need to study these prescriptions and realign our lives and practices with their instruction.

Are we promoting slavery and "the awl through the ear?" No, not at all. We need to look past some of the ancient customs and learn the modern application of the principles of these precepts. While we may not be able to change how our culture designates the names of the days of the week, or the names of the months, we <u>can</u> control what goes on in our homes and churches.

"Christ gave <u>to Moses</u> religious precepts which were to govern the everyday life. These statutes were explicitly given to <u>guard the Ten Commandments</u>. They were not shadowy types to pass away with the death of Christ. They were to be binding upon man in every age as long as time should last. These commands were enforced by

---

[50] *Ibid.,* p. 311.

The Elijah Message

the power of the <u>moral law</u>, and they clearly and definitely explained that law."[51]

"The <u>statutes and judgments</u> specifying the duty of man to his fellow-men, were full of important instruction, defining and simplifying the principles of the <u>moral law</u>, for the purpose of increasing religious knowledge, and of preserving God's chosen people distinct and separate from idolatrous nations."[52]

Here it is clearly revealed that what Christ gave to Moses as statutes and judgments are part of the Moral Law. The statutes and judgments referred to cannot be the Ten Commandments themselves, for these statutes and judgments were given to "guard the Ten Commandments." Something given to "guard the Ten Commandments" cannot themselves be the Ten Commandments.

"The <u>holy law of God</u> is both brief and comprehensive; for it is easily understood and remembered; and yet it is an expression of the will of God. Its comprehensiveness is summed up in the following words: '<u>Thou shalt love the Lord thy God</u> with all thy heart, and with all thy soul, and with all thy mind, and with all thy strength. ... <u>Thou shalt love thy neighbor as thyself</u>.' 'This do, and thou shalt live.' 'Ye shall therefore <u>keep my statutes, and my judgments</u>, which if a man do, he shall live in them; I am the Lord.' 'Cursed be he that confirmeth not all the words of this law."[53]

---

[51] E. G. White, *The Review and Herald*, May 6, 1875.
[52] *Ibid.*
[53] E. G. White, *The Signs of the Times*, September 5, 1892.

62

The Statutes and Judgments

Now we see the structure of the Moral Law:

God is Love

Love God supremely
Love your neighbor impartially

The Ten Commandments

The Statutes and Judgments

The Moral law includes the foundational principles (God is love, love God, love your neighbor), the fundamental precepts (the Ten Commandments) and the "fine print" (the statutes and judgments).

This helps us to understand Exodus 34:28: "And He [God] wrote on the tablets the words of the covenant, the Ten Commandments." Exodus 34 has just recited what God gave as the renewed Covenant. This Covenant contains provisions for mercy and forgiveness. It is based on what God offers to do. It is clearly the Everlasting Covenant. Then it is said that the words of the Covenant are the Ten Commandments. But the words of the Ten Commandments are not what God spoke in Exodus 34.

The relationship between the Ten Commandments and the Covenant of Exodus 34 shows the Ten Commandments are the <u>headlines</u> and the words in Exodus 34:10-26 are the <u>fine print</u> of the Moral Law.

This explains Ezekiel 36:25-27, where it shows the statutes and judgments are part of the New Covenant. This validates the statutes and

The Elijah Message

judgments as part of the Moral Law to be proclaimed as noted in Malachi 4:4. Things are beginning to fit together. Pieces are interlocking. A picture is emerging.

"The very same principles expressed in James 3 were spoken by the voice of God from the pillar of cloud. God spoke to the people the acts they should do and the actions they should not do. Deuteronomy chapter 4. The specifications are never to lose their force, for they are the expression of the mind of the infinite God. Every word is to be cherished."[54]

Turning to Deuteronomy 4 we find: "Listen to the statutes and judgments. ... Keep the commandments of the Lord your God ... I have taught you statutes and judgments, just as the Lord my God commanded me ... be careful to observe them. ... What great nation is there that has such statutes and righteous judgments as are in all this law. ... So He declared to you His covenant which He commanded you to perform, the Ten Commandments; and He wrote them on two tablets of stone. And the Lord commanded me at that time to teach you statutes and judgments, that you might observe them in the land which you cross over to possess." (Deut. 4:1, 2, 5, 8, 13-14).

"God [will] have a clean and holy people to declare His statutes and judgments."[55]

These things are never to lose their force.

---

[54] E. G. White, *1888 Materials*, p. 877. Dairy Entry for January 13, 1891.
[55] E. G. White, *Testimonies for the Church*, Vol. 1, p. 333, c. 1861.

64

Grace and the Law

Now, wait a minute, I can hear someone say, what is all this talk about keeping the law? Doesn't Paul say Jesus has ended the law? Doesn't Paul say we are under grace and no longer under the law?

"Grace is unmerited favor."[56] God loved us while we were yet sinners, and sent Christ to die in our place and forge the path of salvation back to heaven for us. Only someone sent from heaven could provide the way back to heaven. Only Christ could answer the questions of the universe about the badness of sin and the goodness of God. Only Christ, having divine life within Himself, could experience the wages of sin, the wrath of God, which is complete separation from God, and still live long enough to decide if life without God the Father was better or worse than life connected to the Father. Christ experienced this total separation from God as He hung on the cross with the weight of our sins upon Him. If life without God was wonderful, Jesus could have supported His existence separate from God. But He found separation from His Father so excruciating, so agonizing, that He voluntarily chose to end His life, rather than continue to live without connection to His Father.

We see several "layers" of truth in Jesus' sacrifice for humanity. By His death on the cross, Jesus "paid the price" for our sins. He paid the ultimate

---

56 E. G. White, *Selected Messages,* Bk. 1, p. 331.

price, which is the "second death," or total separation from His Father. Jesus became our
"*kapparah*:" our substitutionary sacrifice for at-
one-ment. He died in our place, thus providing the
"ransom" that frees us from our sins and from the
penalty for our sins, which would mean eternal
death. No repentant sinner who accepts the
sacrifice that Jesus Christ made on his behalf need
experience the "wrath of God" (total separation
from God), which results in the "second death" or
eternal death. Jesus experienced the agony of
complete separation from God. Because Jesus
went through this agonizing separation, we can
understand that the ultimate destruction of
wicked, unrepentant sinners is a loving act, and is
consistent with the loving character of God.

Jesus obeyed His Father perfectly during His life
on earth (He did not sin – He had no guilt of
Himself), yet as He took the sinner's place the
guilt of the sins of the entire world were placed
upon Jesus, beginning Thursday night in the
garden of Gethsemane (*Gat Sh'manim:* place of
the oil press). As we see Jesus struggle to bear
the guilt of sin, we begin to understand something
about what rebellious sinners will experience when
they face their guilt at the White Throne Judgment
(Revelation 20:11-15). In the garden, we see
Jesus suffer nearly to the point of dying: "And He
took with Him Peter and the two sons of Zebedee,
and He began to be sorrowful and deeply
distressed. Then He said to them, 'My soul is
exceedingly sorrowful, even to death. Stay here
and watch with Me.' He went a little farther and
fell on His face, and prayed, saying, 'O My Father,
if it is possible, let this cup pass from Me; never-

theless, not as I will, but as You will." Matthew 26:37-39. "And being in agony, He prayed more earnestly. Then His sweat became like great drops of blood falling down to the ground." Luke 22:44.

This agony and distress came on Jesus before his enemies laid a hand on Him. It was the result of the weight of the guilt of the sins of the world, and the struggle Jesus had, knowing that He soon would be separated from His Father as a result of bearing our sins. From Jesus' experience, we can understand the terrible impact of sin, and the guilt that unrepentant sinners will eventually experience.

By bearing our sins, by paying the price for our sins, Jesus nullifies the legal accusations that have been written against us. Every time we sin, Satan keeps a list. He comes into God's courtroom waving this list of accusations against us, and the list is true! But if we repent of our sins and have accepted Jesus' sacrifice in our stead, Jesus steps forward and says, 'That list of sins is no longer valid. I already paid the penalty for those sins.' Thus the power of Satan to accuse us is taken away. Here we see God's grace in action. What a loving and powerful Savior we have!

As Jesus was arrested, tried and cruelly treated, the character of Satan was unmasked. No longer could Satan pose as benign. Now the universe understood the true character of the rebellion that began in heaven. It was so caustic that it resulted in the creature treating his Creator with utmost cruelty.

The Elijah Message

As we contemplate what Jesus went through, we can better understand the insult this treatment was to Jesus. If a man slaps his dog, we might not think much of it. If a man slaps another man, we are disturbed. If a man walks into a courtroom and slaps the judge, we are shocked. If a man walks up and slaps God – what can be said: it is beyond comprehension. But that is what happened to Jesus, only much worse. Satan inspired the most evil treatment of Jesus to convince Jesus to give up the plan of salvation. With every blow, with every lash, Satan was tempting Jesus: Do you love man-kind more than this? You don't have to put up with this! You could zap all these people and go back to heaven. Come down from the cross!

But Jesus showed that His love for humanity exceeded Satan's cruelty. Jesus had exhibited God's love for mankind during His life, and now He exhibited God's love for mankind in His death. Satan was unmasked and could no longer deceive the sinless inhabitants of God's universe. With each blow that Satan inspired, he was assuring his own defeat. By completing the plan of redemption, Jesus assured not only our salvation but also Satan's ultimate demise. The cross shows us how much God loves us, and how much Jesus was willing to go through in order to secure our salvation. Wonderful Savior! Because God loves us this much, we want to do whatever God asks us to do. We will obey God because we love Him.

When we understand the law of God is a transcript of His character - when we realize God's law is the Royal Law, the law of love - we can better understand that Jesus also died in defense of God's law. The law said sinners had to die: "The wages of sin is death." (Romans 6:23).

Because God's law is the foundation of His government, changing God's law would require changing His character and dismantling His government. God's promise is: "My covenant I will not break, nor alter the word that has gone out of My lips." (Psalm 89:34). We see that the death of none less than God the Son could save the sinner. That is how important the law is. If the law could have been changed, Jesus would not have had to die. Paul puts it this way: "Do we then make void the law through faith? Certainly not! On the contrary, we establish the law." (Romans 3:31). Christ's death shows the immutability of God's law.

The law could not be changed, but the penalty could be met. "And Abraham said, 'My son, God will provide for Himself the lamb." (Genesis 22:7). God loved mankind so much that He provided His Lamb – His only Son – to be the sacrifice in our stead, to meet the demands of the unchangeable law.

But some would object: Paul says "Christ is the end of the law!" (Romans 10:4). To understand this text, one needs to understand the underlying Greek word that is translated as "end." The word is *telos,* a word that has the primary meaning of "goal" or "end point." Christ is the culmination of the law, not the abolishment of the law. Christ is the ultimate portrayal of the law.

The Elijah Message

What about: "For sin shall not have dominion over you, for you are not under law but under grace." (Romans 6:14). A beginning glimpse of the practical application of this text is seen in the very next verse: "Shall we sin because we are not under law but under grace? Certainly not!" (Romans 6:15).

The clue to some of these difficult statements Paul makes about "law" comes from an understanding that Paul used the Greek word *nomos* in various ways, to refer to various things. The word *nomos* is a general term for "law" and can refer to civil law, or religious law, natural law or even "ultimate truth principle."

Let me explain. In several places in his writings, Paul explains three aspects of the sin problem and its solution, in stepwise fashion. An example of this is Romans 6:15-7:12. First, Paul establishes that we are born under the law of carnality, as slaves to sin. This is an "ultimate truth principle" – it is "how things are." When Adam sinned, he lost his robe of light (representing his holy, spiritual nature) and gained a carnal nature prone to sin. Ever since Adam's fall, mankind has been having trouble with this sinful, carnal nature. Because we have sinful carnal natures (natures with a "bent" to sin), we are easy marks for Satan's temptations and deceptions. It is a lot easier for us to sin than to live pure and holy lives. Then, in Romans 6:23a, Paul establishes the results of sinning: "The wages of sin is death." This is another "ultimate truth principle" that Paul subsequently refers to as *nomos* or "law." (See Romans 8:2).

But Paul quickly juxtaposes the solution: "The gift of God is eternal life in Christ Jesus our Lord." (Romans 6:23b). This is God's law of grace. In neither instance is Paul referring to the Moral Law. He is talking about the law of carnality vs the law of grace. We are born under the law of carnality (we have sinful natures with a "bent" to sin), but God offers salvation to us by grace, through the sacrificial gift of Jesus Christ.

Paul continues in Romans 7:1-6, explaining that we have the choice to be under the law of carnality or under the law of grace. He uses the law of marriage as an illustration: while a husband lives, his wife is bound by the moral law to be faithful to him. But if the husband dies, the wife is released from her marriage vows and can legitimately (according to the moral law) remarry someone else. Paul points out that at baptism we are to die to our "old man of sin" as we are buried in the waters of baptism. This is "circumcision of the heart" spoken of in Deut. 10:16. If we are dead to our "old man of sin," we no longer respond to our sinful carnal nature, which is the "access point" for the devil's temptations and deceptions. We have been freed from the "law of carnality" and now enjoy the freedom of the law of grace.

Paul strongly points out that the freedom of the law of grace is not license to sin! (Romans 6:18). Just the opposite: the law of grace frees us from the power of sin in our lives.

How does this work? Many people misunderstand grace because they focus only on Part I of grace:

The Elijah Message

By grace through faith in Jesus Christ we receive pardon for our sins. This is justification, or Part I of grace. Part I of grace puts us in right relation to God's law, because we have been forgiven and are no longer condemned by God's law. But there is more to grace than pardon. Grace is also God's power to change our lives and make us into new creatures. This is sanctification, or Part II of God's grace. Through the power of the Holy Spirit in our lives, we become transformed. This is a process, not an instant event. This is Christian growth in Christ. The robe of Christ's righteousness that we receive at justification not only covers us and presents us to God as though we had never sinned, it also works to cleanse us of all unright-eousness. This cleansing not only removes past guilt, but gives us the power to not sin in the future. Thus the grace of God not only <u>puts</u> us into right relationship with His law through pardon at justification, but it also <u>keeps</u> us in right relation-ship (obedience) with His law through sanctifica-tion. Christ justifies us through the cleansing power of His blood, and He sanctifies us (empow-ers obedience) through the working of the Holy Spirit in our lives. Both justification and sanctifica-tion are gifts of God's grace.

As we live the Christian life, we grow up into Christ. It is a gradual process, and sometimes we are taken over the same road more than once. Success comes when we learn to submit our ways to God through the Holy Spirit. When we are confronted with the ugly head of self, we are to submit to the working of the Holy Spirit. Too often we want to have things our way, and we fret and fuss if things don't go as we would like. Or we are willfully disobedient, doing those things we know we shouldn't, simply because of the appealing nature of sin. Often we are struggling with ingrained habit patterns, and the battle is long and the struggle severe as we learn new ways of functioning according to God's plan. But step by step the Holy Spirit will continue to remind us and empower us to act according to God's will.

Paul also used the term *Upos nomon* ("under the law") to refer to "earned righteousness" or legalism. The problem with legalism is that it doesn't work. First, in our own strength we are no match for our sinful carnal natures. Only Christ through the Holy Spirit can subdue our carnal natures and empower us to live righteous, obedient lives. Secondly, we cannot do anything to make God love us more – He already loved us supremely before we ever knew about Him. Thirdly, our best efforts fall far short of perfect obedience, and only perfect obedience (past, present and future) can meet the demands of the law. Christ's perfect righteousness is the only righteousness that perfectly meets the pure and holy standards of God's law, and this righteousness He gives to us freely. It is only through God's grace that we are justified, and it is only through God's grace that we are sanctified. We need a Savior! That Savior is Jesus Christ.

"It is impossible for us, of ourselves, to escape from the pit of sin in which we are sunken. Our hearts are evil, and we cannot change them. 'Who can bring a clean thing out of an unclean? Not one.' [Job 14:4]. 'The carnal mind is enmity against God: for it is not subject to the law of God,

73

neither indeed can be.' [Romans 8:7]. Education, culture, the exercise of the will, human effort, all have their proper sphere, but here they are powerless. They may produce an outward correctness of behavior, but they cannot change the heart; they cannot purify the springs of life. There must be a power working from within, a new life from above, before men can be changed from sin to holiness. That power is Christ. His grace alone can quicken the lifeless faculties of the soul, and attract it to God, to holiness."[57]

We have shown the principles that are the foundation of God's law: 1) God is love; 2) Love God supremely; 3) Love your neighbor impartially. Not many would argue with love! The law is simply God's explanation about what love is. The moral law shows us the particulars of what it means to love God supremely and to love our neighbor impartially.

Is it the function of God's grace to "hand us over" to sin? Absolutely not! Jesus died to give us freedom from sin and sinning. When we understand that sin is our enemy, then we will value the gift of grace that results in obedience to God's law. Through the power imparted to us by the Holy Spirit, with changed hearts and minds, we will obey God's law because we love God and we know God loves us. We understand that His way of living is the best way there is.

As we become obedient to God's law, we participate in God's will for us. Christ becomes our

---

[57] E. G. White, *Steps to Christ*, p. 18.

companion through the Holy Spirit. Living God's way brings love, hope, peace and joy. We become citizens of the heavenly kingdom, as the kingdom is established in our hearts. We are preparing for the joys of heaven, for we experience fellowship with heaven here on earth. Rightly understood, there is no conflict between obedience to the law and relationship with Jesus Christ, for they both emanate from the same source.

A note about Galatians 4:8-11: An honest reading of this section reveals Paul is speaking about the Galatian believers returning to (vs 9) the "days, months, seasons [times] and years" (vs. 10) associated with the "beggarly elements" of "bondage" (vs. 9) of the "no gods" (vs 8). The Galatians were Gentile believers who were former pagans (vs 8). Paul never referred to the Lords' Feasts of Leviticus 23 as "beggarly elements." Paul never referred to God as a "no god." To say this is what Paul meant is to twist the meaning of the text.

In Galatians 4:8-11 Paul is shocked that the Gentile believers are turning once again to the pagan holidays. Such holidays can be traced back to the Tower of Babel. These heathen times are spoken against in Deuteronomy 18:9-14: "There shall not be found among you anyone that maketh his son or his daughter to pass through the fire, or that useth divinations, or an observer of times, or an enchanter, or a witch. ... But as for thee, the Lord thy God hath not suffered thee so to do." (Deut. 18:10, 14).

True vs False Jews

"And to the angel of the church in Smyrna write, These things says the First and the Last, who was dead, and came to life: 'I know your works, tribulation, and poverty (but you are rich); and I know the blasphemy of those who say they are Jews and are not, but are a congregation of Satan. Do not fear any of those things which you are about to suffer." (Revelation 2:8-10).

This text says there are those who claim to be Jews (this is positive) but are not (this is negative) – these false pretenders are of the congregation of Satan and persecute those who are true Jews.

That this was written to the church at Smyrna is significant, in light of what we have studied about Polycarp, Christian bishop at Smyrna in the early 2nd century AD, and what happened to him. He was persecuted by those in Rome who called themselves Christians but who were incorporating pagan practices into their worship. To blaspheme is to set oneself in God's place or in opposition to God. By 150 AD the apostate Christians at Rome retained Christ's name, while their practice was opposed to Christ's true religion.

Further light is shed on this subject by Rev. 5:5: "But one of the elders said to me, 'Do not weep. Behold, the Lion of the tribe of Judah, the Root of David, has prevailed to open the scroll and to loose its seven seals." Of whom is the elder speaking? "And I looked, and behold, in the midst of the throne and of the four living creatures, and in the midst of the elders, stood a Lamb as though it had been slain." (vs. 6) This can be none other than Jesus Christ. He is both the slain Lamb and the Lion of the tribe of Judah.

A lion is a common symbol of a king. Here, Jesus is called a King. The King of whom? The King of the tribe of Judah – today we use the same root word (*Y'hudah*) for the word "Jew." Here, in Rev. 5:5, Jesus Christ, the Lamb that was slain, is given the appellation "King of the Jews."

When Christ was crucified, Pilate commanded a sign be placed above His head on the cross. A sign was often placed on the crosses of criminals to designate their guilt – the infraction of the law for which they were being punished. The sign over the head of Jesus Christ, in three languages, read: "Jesus of Nazareth, the King of the Jews." (John 19:19). To accommodate the limited space on such a sign, especially when written in three languages, the practice was often followed of listing only the first letter of each word – what we today call an acronym. In Hebrew the sign would read, "*Yeshuah HaNazaret V'Melech HaY'hudah.*"

Shortened to an acronym that would read:

YHVH

As John records: "Then many of the Jews read this title. ... Therefore the chief priests of the Jews said to Pilate, 'Do not write, "The King of the Jews," but, "He said, 'I am the King of the Jews." (John 19:20-21). But Pilate refused to change the sign.

The Elijah Message

In Revelation 5:5 Jesus Christ is proclaimed to be the King of the Jews, the True Jew. Not only that, "Jesus was the originator of the religion of the Jews."[58] If we want to know Christ's religion, we must not ignore what was given to Moses for Israel. Paul points out the family to which believers in Jesus Christ belong: "And if you are Christ's, then you are Abraham's seed, and heirs according to the promise." (Gal. 3:29). When we belong to Christ, He adopts us into the family of Abraham – we become grafted-in branches on the Olive Tree of Israel. But there is a caution! "Do not boast against the branches. But if you do boast, remember that you do not support the root, but the root supports you. You will say then, 'Branches were broken off that I might be grafted in.' Well said. Because of unbelief they were broken off, and you stand by faith. Do not be haughty, but fear. For if God did not spare the natural branches, He may not spare you either. ... And they also, if they do not continue in unbelief, will be grafted in, for God is able to graft them in again. For if you were cut out of the olive tree which is wild by nature, and were grafted contrary to nature into a cultivated olive tree, how much more will these, who are natural branches, be grafted into their own olive tree?" (Romans 11:18-21, 23-24).

All branches on the Olive Tree are there by faith in Messiah and are obedient to the Covenant given to Abraham by the Messiah. While many natural branches fell away through unbelief, there remained a faithful remnant: those believing Jews who remained branches through faith in Jesus Christ.

---

[58] E. G. White, *The Signs of the Times,* November 7, 1892.

"The middle wall of partition between the Jew and Gentile was broken down. They were no longer in separate rooms; the unbelieving Gentile [that was his history] has been united with the believing Jew. The Gentile did not crowd the Jews from their original position, but he became a partaker with them of their blessings."[59] As Gentiles come to a belief in Jesus Christ, they become part of the family of Abraham, and are grafted by faith into the Olive Tree of Israel.

Jesus taught, "If you abide in My word, you are My disciples indeed. And you shall know the truth, and the truth shall make you free." (John 8:31-32).

This was shocking to the Pharisees, for it proclaimed the freedom of individual conscience to discover and follow truth. The Pharisees held that only the sages could understand truth, and all the common people had to learn truth, not directly from the Scriptures, but from the writings and commentary of the rabbis.

Jesus was very clear: "I speak what I have seen with My Father, and you do what you have seen with your father.' They answered and said to Him, 'Abraham is our father.' Jesus said to them, 'If you were Abraham's children, you would do the works of Abraham." (John 8:38-39). What did Abraham do? "Abraham obeyed My voice and kept My charge, My commandments, My statutes, and My laws." (Genesis 26:5).

When Christ adopts us into the family of Abraham, we happily do the things Abraham did, for they are

---

[59] E. G. White, The Signs of the Times, August 25, 1887.

The Elijah Message

the things that Christ commanded Moses, and they are the things Christ Himself practiced. We become "grafted in" to the Olive Tree of Israel – grafted in "among them" – among the faithful Israelites who derive righteousness from Jesus Christ, and practice loving obedience as taught in the *Torah*. (See Romans 11:16-24).

Some would point to Romans 10:4 and say, "See, the law has ended – Christ brought an end to the law." This is a misconstruing of the meaning of the text. In Romans 10:4, the word "end" comes from the Greek word *telos* meaning goal or culmination. Christ is the culmination of the law. Christ did not end the Moral law. Christ is the source of the *Torah* that nourishes the Olive Tree. Christ is the source of right-doing for all the branches on the Olive Tree: "Christ is the culmination of the law, for righteousness to everyone who believes." (Romans 10:4). If you go down through the branches of the Olive Tree, down through the trunk of the tree, down through the roots (*Torah*), at the tips of the roots, there you find Christ. Christ is the source of nourishment for all believers who are true Jews – followers of the True Jew.

Revelation 2:9 clearly points out the apostasy of the Christian church in the centuries after Christ. The false Christians brought in pagan practices – they became part of the "congregation of Satan." But if there were false Jews (false Christians), this means that faithful Christians such as those in Smyrna were true Jews – followers of the True Jew: Jesus Christ.

"'Not every one that saith unto me, Lord, Lord, shall enter into the kingdom of Heaven; but he that doeth the will of my Father which is in heaven.' [Matt. 7:21]. What is the will of the Father? That we keep His commandments. Christ, to enforce the will of his Father, became the author of the statutes and precepts given <u>through Moses</u> to the people of God. Christians who extol Christ, but array themselves against the law governing the Jewish church, array Christ against Christ."[60]

"The New Testament is not a new religion, and the Old Testament is not a religion to be superseded by the New. The New Testament is only the advancement and unfolding of the Old."[61]

Here is the distinction: we are to follow the religion of the Bible (Old and New Testaments in unfolding truth), and we are to accept nothing that does not have a "Thus saith the Lord" behind it. Unfortunately, many who call themselves Christians accept what the apostasy so many years ago brought into the Christian church. They and their pastors have practiced these things for so long, they don't even think about it. After all, are not these things called by Christ's name? Are they not said to be symbolic of events in Christ's life? What many people do not realize is that Satan has his religion that competes with Christ's religion. The two are not to be amalgamated. It takes only a little dirt to make clean water unfit to drink. It takes only a little here and there of things that have origins in paganism to contaminate Christ's

---

[60] E. G. White, *The Review and Herald*, May 6, 1875.
[61] E. G. White, *Special Testimonies to Ministers*, No. 3, p. 40-41.

The Elijah Message

religion. We must not be fooled by false religion. In the end times, Satan will appear as an angel of light (looking like a heavenly/divine being) calling himself Christ and will deceive many. Those who stand against him, accepting only what is taught as Christ's religion in the Bible, will be called anti-Christ, because they do not bow to this false Christ. Are we prepared for that? Or by following the pagan days and ways brought into the church years ago, are we preparing ourselves to worship the one who originated these pagan practices?

"As the storm approaches, a large class who have professed faith in the third angel's message, but have not been sanctified through obedience to the truth, abandon their position and join the ranks of the opposition. By uniting with the world and partaking of its spirit, they have come to view matters in nearly the same light; and when the test is brought, they are prepared to choose the easy, popular side."[62]

Those who bury their heads in the sand now are determining their own fate during the time of testing. May God keep us alert and aware, and obedient to the truths of the Bible.

---

[62] E. G. White, *The Great Controversy*, p. 608, 1888.

The Elijah Message

We now come full circle to the Elijah message. To understand Malachi 4:4-5 we need to study the work of Elijah the prophet. Elijah first appears in 1 Kings 17:1, bringing the prediction of drought to Ahab, king of the northern tribes.

The story really begins some 60 years before King Ahab: After Israel split into two kingdoms upon the death of Solomon, the northern kingdom quickly slid into apostasy. King Jeroboam had the word of the Lord that he was the one chosen to rule over the northern tribes, but his faith was weak and he was determined to keep his people away from Jerusalem where they might become attached to Rehoboam the son of Solomon. To accomplish this, Jeroboam came up with a method to keep the people from attending the annual Pilgrim feasts. He set up golden calf idols at Dan and Bethel, and told the people, "Behold thy gods, O Israel, which brought thee up out of the land of Egypt." (1 Kings 12:28). The language of the text is shockingly like Exodus 32:4. To further confuse things, Jeroboam established his own festival calendar. Thus the king brought God's swift rebuke upon himself and his people.

Scripture is clear about Jeroboam's worship: "Then he [Jeroboam] appointed for himself priests for the high places, for the demons, and the calf idols which he had made." (2 Chron. 11:15). "The king's bold defiance of God in thus setting aside divinely appointed institutions was not allowed to pass unrebuked."[63] What institutions did Jeroboam set aside? He set aside the Pilgrim Feasts of Passover, *Shavuot*/Pentecost and Tabernacles.

The prophet of the Lord appeared while Jeroboam was offering sacrifices to his golden calf idol. At the prophet's rebuke, Jeroboam defiantly ordered the prophet held. Jeroboam's hand that was stretched out, pointing at the prophet, became shriveled, while the idol altar was rent asunder and the ashes poured out upon the ground. Terror-stricken, Jeroboam begged the prophet to pray for him, that his hand might be restored. God answered the prophet's prayer and Jeroboam's hand was restored, but he did not learn the desired lesson. Israel continued its slide into apostasy.

By the time of Elijah, the situation was about as low as it could get. Jeroboam's idolatry had been "home-grown," but king Ahab brought in professionals! He married Jezebel, the daughter of a priest of Baal who was also king of the Sidonians (1 Kings 16:31). When Jezebel arrived at the palace in Samaria, she brought with her 400 prophets of Ashtoreth and 450 prophets of Baal (also known as Molech). "And Ahab made an Asherah image. Ahab did more to provoke the Lord God of Israel to anger than all the kings of Israel who were before him." (1 Kings 16:33). If we want to know what God thinks of Easter, we need only read what He thinks of Ashtoreth, for they trace back to the same thing. To get an idea of what the worship of Ashtoreth entailed, we

---

[63] E. G. White, *Prophets and Kings,* p. 101, 1917.

need only read about Diana of the Ephesians. Ashtoreth, Diana, Venus, Isis, Aphrodite, Easter -- all trace back to Ishtar, the fertility goddess of Babylonian sun worship.

The pagan worship under Ahab and Jezebel is described: "Captivated by the gorgeous display and the fascinating rites of idol worship, the people followed the example of the king and his court, and gave themselves up to the intoxicating, degrading pleasures of a sensual worship."[64]

Descriptions of such elaborate rites were written by the ancients regarding their secret demon worship, including fascinating light shows and the apparitions of persons known to be dead.[65]

Paul warned: "The things which the Gentiles sacrifice they sacrifice to demons and not to God, and I do not want you to have fellowship with demons. You cannot drink the cup of the Lord and the cup of demons; you cannot partake of the Lord's table and of the table of demons." (1 Corinth. 10:20-21). While Paul clearly states: "idols are nothing," (see vs. 19), yet the force behind idols is demon worship. Those religious practices that originated in the mind of Satan remain his avenue to trick and entrap men. This includes Satan's religious calendar. Those who ignore this warning walk on dangerous ground.

Satan loves to be worshipped as though he is God. (Isaiah 14:13-14). It is possible even for Christians to walk on Satan's ground and worship Satan

---

[64] Ibid., p. 116.
[65] See Alexander Hislop, The Two Babylons, pp. 66-68.

The Elijah Message

as lord. "If men and women who have the knowledge of the truth are so far separated from their
great Leader that they will take the great leader of
apostasy and name him Christ our Righteousness,
it is because they have not sunk deep into the
mines of the truth."[66] It is only the truths of the
Word of God, impressed upon our minds by the
Holy Spirit, that can keep us from such apostasy.

We now have a feel for the level of apostasy that
permeated Israel under the leadership of Ahab and
Jezebel – the apostasy that Elijah confronted.
Under the mandate of the Lord, Elijah boldly
strode into Ahab's court and announced the
upcoming disaster: No rain for an unknown period
of time! The heavens turned to brass above them,
and the earth became barren under their feet. The
food supplies dwindled. Water was in short supply.
The cattle and the children were perishing. After
years of drought, the situation became desperate.

Ahab searched for the prophet who had brought
such doom on the land. But God preserved Elijah,
first beside the brook Cherith, then by sending him
to the widow of Zarephath in Sidon – out of the
country.

Eventually, Elijah returned to Israel and revealed
himself to captain Obadiah, who was less than
happy to receive the prophet. Elijah had proven so
elusive in the past, Obadiah was afraid Elijah
would slip away again and he would be seen as
bearing false news to Ahab.

---

[66] E. G. White, *Selected Messages*, Book 2, (from a statement c.
1897).

The Elijah Message

When Elijah and Ahab did meet, the accusation from the king's lips was, "Is that you, O troubler of Israel?" (1 Kings 18:17). Talk about projection! The guilty accused the innocent!

Elijah then instructed Ahab to call all Israel to a contest between worship systems, to take place on Mt. Carmel. Also to be present were the 400 prophets of Ashtoreth and the 450 prophets of Baal who had been well-fed and supported during the drought, eating at Jezebel's table.

When the people had gathered on Mt. Carmel, Elijah challenged them with: "'How long will you falter between two opinions? If the Lord is God, follow Him; but if Baal, follow him.' But the people answered him not a word." (1 Kings 18:21).

After setting out the rules for the day, the contest began. The false priests were given ample opportunity to make contact with their god, but no answer came. Even brutish blood-letting got no response from the brazen heavens. Elijah carefully monitored the process, allowing no sleight of hand to kindle a fire under the pagan sacrifice.

After the pagan priests had given up, Elijah did a strange thing. He had 12 containers of water brought and poured over the sacrifice on the altar of the Lord. "And it came to pass, at the time of the offering of the evening sacrifice, that Elijah the prophet came near and said, 'Lord God of Abraham, Isaac and Israel, let it be known this day that You are God in Israel and I am Your servant, and that I have done all these things at Your word. Hear me, O Lord, hear me, that this

The Elijah Message

people may know that You are the Lord God, and that You have turned their hearts back to You again.' Then the fire of the Lord fell and consumed the burnt sacrifice, and the wood and the stones and the dust, and it licked up the water that was in the trench. Now when all the people saw it, they fell on their faces; and they said, 'The Lord, He is God! The Lord, He is God!" (1 Kings 18:36-39).

The people were convinced by the overwhelming display of God's power. It's too bad they had not been convinced by the truth of the Scriptures.

Elijah and the people then disposed of the pagan priests of Baal and Ashtoreth. When Jezebel heard what happened, she was furious and vowed to destroy Elijah, just as he had destroyed her priests. Imagine that! One prophet was mightier, with God's help, than 850 pagan priests, and Jezebel still couldn't see the truth. She was determined to maintain her power and position, she refused to change her view or her worship practices, and she thought to destroy the prophet of the Lord.

Isn't that how it so often is? If we don't like the message, we work to destroy the messenger. Too many refuse to submit their way to the truth taught in Scripture. They are determined to remain popular with their friends, even if this requires maintaining a false system.

We need to seriously ask: Who is our Lord? Do we have any comprehension why this matters?

There is another "Elijah" mentioned in Scripture, who also brought an "Elijah message" to the people. Reading the verse in Malachi 4:4-5, the people of Israel had long looked for Elijah to come and prepare the way for the Messiah.

When John the Baptist came preaching the way of the Lord, the people asked him, "'Are you Elijah?' He said, 'I am not.' 'Are you the Prophet?' and he answered, 'No.'" (John 1:21).

Jesus, however, said, "'Elijah is coming first and will restore all things. But I say to you that Elijah has come already, and they did not know him but did to him whatever they wished. Likewise the Son of Man is also about to suffer at their hands.' Then the disciples understood that He spoke to them of John the Baptist." (Matthew 17:11-13).

John the Baptist explained his work as "The voice of one crying in the wilderness: Make straight the way of the Lord." (John 1:23). The text he referenced is Isaiah 40:3 that says: "Make straight in the desert a highway for our God. Every valley shall be exalted and every mountain and hill brought low; the crooked places shall be made straight, and the rough places smooth. The glory of the Lord shall be revealed, and all flesh shall see it together; for the mouth of the Lord has spoken." (Isaiah 40:3-5). Here is prophesied the work of Elijah in the end times. The people must be prepared to receive the Lord when He comes in glory. There are things that have been exalted that need to be brought down. Things that have been suppressed need to be lifted up. There are crooked doings that need to be straightened out. Rough, un-Christlike places need to be made smooth. Everything needs to be brought into conformity with the will and the Word of God.

The Elijah Message

This is both an individual and a corporate process.
The whole system must be examined and brought
into conformity to God's revealed will. The voices
for reform may seem to "cry from the wilderness,"
but those in places of power and prestige do well
to listen. Perhaps they are too close to the
problem. Perhaps they are hanging onto popular
fable and tradition that is not supported by
Scripture. Perhaps they are focused on maintaining their prestige with persons of influence rather
than practicing total dedication to the ways of
God. Perhaps the sparkle and the tinsel have
blinded their eyes. Perhaps they say, "I am rich,
and increased with goods, and have need of
nothing." Perhaps they tell themselves, "We have
the truth, the whole truth and nothing but the
truth. We teach from the Bible. We maintain the
teachings and practices of our forefathers."

"Much has been lost because our ministers and
people have concluded that we have had all the
truth essential for us as a people; but such a
conclusion is erroneous and in harmony with the
deceptions of Satan; for truth will be constantly
unfolding."[67]

The message of Elijah confronted false worship
and re-established true worship among God's
people who had been led into idolatry, even
though in the beginning it was posited as being
the worship of God.

The message of John the Baptist confronted the
mass of human tradition that had buried God's
truth. He pointed people to the simplicity of God's

---

[67] E. G. White, *The Signs of the Times*, May 26, 1890.

90

true religion. He focused on how people should treat their fellow men. He did not fail to expose the hypocrisy of the religious leaders of his day. He exemplified total dedication to his God. Because of his faithful work, he was privileged to introduce the Messiah, the Lamb of God, to the people. His faithful rebuke of sins in high places ultimately cost him his life.

The message of Elijah as portrayed in Malachi 4:4 is: "Remember the Law of Moses My servant, which I commanded him in Mt. Horeb for all Israel, with the statutes and judgments."

We have taken a look at the validity of the Law of Moses, its true Author, and the relationship of the statutes and judgments to the Moral Law.

Will we embrace the challenge? Are we willing to study the principles taught in the Law of Moses and incorporate them into our lives? Shall we determine today to be faithful to the Lord, as He reveals His truth to us? What hills and valleys, crooked and rough places in our lives need to be dealt with? What about those religious practices that are familiar and comfortable, but which came from a source other than Scripture, and represent the deception of the enemy? Are we willing to reform? Or are there parts of our lives that we keep separate and apart from God's direction? There is a specific message given for the end times, and it is found in Revelation 14:6-12. The first angel proclaims the Gospel ("good news"), saying: Worship God and give Him glory, for the hour of His judgment has come. The second angel proclaims: Babylon, that fornicator of religion, will

The Elijah Message

be destroyed. The third angel brings the message: Do not participate in false worship and receive the mark of the beast, or you will be destroyed by the glory of the Lord. Rather, keep the command- ments of God and hold to the testimony of Jesus.

Revelation 18:1-5 is the final message: Come out of Babylon, for those who partake of Babylon will be destroyed along with Babylon. These messages are all about worship: Worship God in the way He specifies, for if you bow to the Babylonish religion you will receive its fate. The false worship days and ways that crept into the Christian church during the 2nd, 3rd and 4th centuries originated in Babylonish sun worship. These stand in opposition to Christ's religion as revealed in Scripture.

By comparing the work and message of Elijah the prophet, the work and message of John the Baptist, and the last warning message to be given at the end of time (Revelation 14:6-12; Revelation 18:1-5) the issues should be crystal clear.

A verse in Romans 6 pertains: "Do you not know that to whom you present yourselves servants to obey, you are that one's servant whom you obey, whether of sin leading to death, or of obedience leading to righteousness?" (Romans 6:16). What are the stakes? Whose side are we on?

The Prophetic Role
of Ellen G. White

You may have noticed that we have included quotations from "E. G. White." Who was she and why do we give her such prominence?[68]

Ellen G. Harmon was born in 1827 into the family of a Methodist hat maker. Her family came to believe in the Millerite message of Christ's second coming on October 22, 1844. At the age of 16, she was bitterly disappointed when Christ did not return on that date.

Later that same year, after she had turned 17, Ellen received her first vision – a view of the people of God climbing up a narrow path, high above the world, leading to the kingdom of God. Over the next 70 years, she received some 2000 visions. During these visions she was found to not breathe, even though she would at times speak, and many of the visions lasted for an hour or longer. Many of her early visions occurred in public group meetings, where she was examined by many people, including physicians, and found to be in a state that normally would not support life. During these visions she was exceedingly strong. Men could not hold her arm from moving, nor could they make her arm move, against what she was doing as part of the vision.

---

[68] The published writings of Ellen G. White may be accessed at www.whiteestate.org

The Elijah Message

Three months before she turned 19, Ellen Harmon married James White, a young minister who had also been part of the Millerite movement and had gone through the great disappointment of 1844. Together they traveled - comforting, encouraging and instructing those who accepted the Sanctuary in Heaven view, and eventually came to accept the validity of the seventh-day Sabbath.

Over the years, the Lord revealed to Ellen White many things about the course of sin through the ages, the history of Israel, and the development of the Christian church. Much of what she was shown fits into the theme of the Great Controversy – the struggle between Christ and Satan since rebellion entered the universe in the mind of Lucifer.

The validity of the Law of God is a strong focus in her writings. She understood the Law as the transcript of God's character. Christ came as the embodiment of God's law, showing God's love to man and how God's law could be obeyed through Christ's power. Christ magnified the law and made it honorable (Isaiah 42:21), and we are to do the same. We are not to teach the law apart from Christ, but rather teach Christ in the law.

Health topics were the subject of some of Ellen White's visions. It has been said that what she wrote about health was 100 years ahead of her time. Although some of what she wrote was being taught by various health reformers of her day, she had an uncanny ability to accept the true and reject the false. Thus her writings on health have stood the test of time, unlike much of what was written by her contemporaries.

Ellen G. White, the Prophet

Ellen White was shown the things that will happen during the time of the end – that fascinating and terrible time just before the second coming of Christ. We do well to understand what she wrote, for it is a map for the future. She saw the need for character development in God's children. She saw our utter dependence upon Christ for both justification and sanctification. She saw the work of Christ in the heavenly sanctuary, as He pleads His blood on our behalf. She saw the closing of probationary time, when all will have decided either for or against God's truth, and all cases will have been sealed for eternal life or eternal damnation. She saw the time of trouble when the seven last plagues will fall upon the wicked. She saw the sheltering covering and protection of heavenly angels that God will provide for His faithful during the falling of the plagues.

Remember those "divinely appointed institutions" that Jeroboam set aside? Ellen White had more to say about them: "In the time of the end, every divine institution is to be restored."[69] She points out "The breach made in the law at the time the Sabbath was changed by man, is to be repaired."[70] This is a prophetic statement that pertains to the time of the end. Are we living in the last days? Then this prophecy is for us!

As we have studied this topic, it has become clear that not only the Sabbath was changed, but all of God's holy times were changed by nominal Christianity. This was predicted by the prophet

---

[69] E. G. White, *Prophets and Kings*, p. 678, 1917.
[70] *Ibid*.

The Elijah Message

Daniel: "And he shall think to change <u>times</u> [plural] and law." (Daniel 7:25). This would happen before the "Great Persecution" for the text says, "<u>Then</u> the saints shall be given into his hand for a time and times and half a time."

Note the text says "times" will be changed. These are "times" associated with God's law. And certainly, as we have seen, more than one "time" commanded in God's law has been changed. Most Christians have completely thrown out God's "times" and have accepted the false "times" that were brought into the Christian church during the 2nd to 4th centuries. Few Christians today are even aware of the issues. Everything has been piled high with church custom and tradition; pagan aspects have been given Christian names, and most Christians have no idea of the source of things they practice.

Two men can have the same name, be born in the same year, live in the same county, work for the same company – but if they have different parents, they are not the same person. To distinguish the true from the false often takes some detective work. It also requires belief in what one finds, and the willingness to act upon it. Those who sit with hands folded will never act upon the truth.

We must be like Ezra and Nehemiah – dedicated to restoring the Book of the Law – the *Torah* – the Word of God into our lives. We do ourselves a disservice when we throw away half of the Bible, or parse a chapter into verses we accept and verses we ignore.

We must be like Josiah, who was proceeding with reform as best he knew, when the Book of the Law was found in the run-down temple. When it was read, and he understood how far his people had apostatized, he tore his clothes and wept. But he did not stop there. He began tearing down the places of pagan worship and even went up into northern Israel, a nearly vacant land since the northern tribes had been taken off into captivity, so that the entire land would be rid of this offense to God. It was Josiah who fulfilled the prophecy against the pagan altar of Jeroboam.

Do we know what the divine institutions are? They are clearly identified. They were thrown aside by Jeroboam (see 1 Kings 12:26-33). They were abolished by the Council of Nicea in 325 AD. We now know that in both instances, the Feasts of the Lord were cast aside. These are clearly included in the "divine institutions" that are to be restored "in the time of the end." In Ellen White's day, the emphasis was on the restoration of the seventh-day Sabbath (see Leviticus 23:1-3). In the time of the end, the remaining "divine institutions" are to be restored.

Malachi 4:4-5 states: "Remember the Law of Moses ... with the statutes and judgments. Behold, I will send you Elijah the prophet before the coming of the great and dreadful day of the Lord." The Elijah message of the last days includes the statutes and judgments. Elijah wrote no book nor did he make any far-reaching prophecies. The work of Elijah was to confront false worship and call the people back to the true worship of God. Coupled with Revelation 14:6-12 and Revelation

The Elijah Message

18:1-5, we see that the Elijah message confronts the false worship promoted by Babylon.

God's system of worship and Satan's system of worship are in opposition to each other. This is that last great battle of the Great Controversy – the battle over worship. The Law of Moses with the statutes and judgments stands in opposition to pagan days and ways.

God's worship system includes the seventh-day Sabbath, Passover, Early Firstfruits, Pentecost, Trumpets, Atonement and Tabernacles (see Leviticus 23). Babylon's worship system includes the Venerable Day of the Sun, Easter Sunday, Lent, Cupid's day, Halloween, December 25 and others. We must not think that mixing the two systems together is acceptable to God. God calls us out of Babylon, to learn His ways and be sanctified totally to Him. When we turn toward God, we are to turn our back on paganism. When we worship at the pagan altar, we turn our back on God. When we follow what originated in the mind of Satan, putting Christ's name on Satan's days and ways, we are calling Satan "Christ our Righteousness."

"The gospel is given in precept in Leviticus. Implicit obedience is required now, as then. How important it is that we understand the importance of this word! Only two classes will be developed in this world – the obedient and the disobedient."[71] There are two systems in Leviticus that show the gospel: the animal sacrificial system and the

---

[71] E. G. White, *Special Testimonies to Ministers*, No. 3, p. 41, 1895.

Ellen G. White, the Prophet

Feasts of the Lord whose themes focus on the gospel. One of these systems is still to be obeyed.

While there is much talk about our "mission," we must not forget the <u>message</u>: "The disciples were to teach what Christ had taught. That which He had spoken, not only in person, but through all the prophets and teachers of the Old Testament, is here included. Human teaching is shut out. There is no place for tradition, for man's theories and conclusions, or for church legislation. No laws ordained by ecclesiastical authority are included in the commission. ... <u>Nothing</u> that does not bear His [Christ's] superscription is to be recognized in His kingdom."[72]

Regarding the Book of the Law found in the days of Josiah, we read, "In Josiah's day the Word of the Lord was as binding, and should have been as strictly enforced, as at the time it was spoken. And today it is as binding as it was then. God is always true to His Word."[73]

God does not forget His word. He will bring it to pass. The question is, will we be for God or will we be against Him. How long will we halt between two opposing choices?

---

[72] E. G. White, *The Desire of Ages,* p. 826, 1898.
[73] E. G. White, *General Conference Bulletin,* April 1903.

Scripture Index

Scripture Index

The Elijah Message

Luke 22:44	67	Acts 2:7-8	41
John 1:18	5	Acts 2:13	41
John 1:21	89	Acts 10:6	11
John 1:23	89	Acts 15	18, 22
John 2:13	39	Acts 15:19-21	19
John 2:14-19	40	Acts 16:3	23
John 2:16	41	Acts 18:21	11
John 3:16	39	Acts 18:21	39
John 3:16	74	Acts 20:6	11
John 4:21, 23	21	Acts 20:6	39
John 4:21-24	39	Acts 20:16	11
John 5:1	39	Acts 21:21	23
John 6	39	Acts 28:17	23
John 6	40	Romans 2:28-29	23
John 6:4	39	Romans 3:31	8
John 6:46	5	Romans 3:31	69
John 6:59	39	Romans 6:14	70
John 7:10	39	Romans 6:15	70
John 7:10-39	40	Rom. 6:15-7:12	70
John 7:37-38	40	Romans 6:15-23	70
John 8:31-32	79	Romans 6:16	92
John 8:38-39	79	Romans 6:23	9
John 10:22-23	39	Romans 6:23	69
John 12:1	39	Romans 6:23	70-71
John 12:24	37	Romans 7:1-6	71
John 13:26	34	Romans 7:12	8
John 13:36	34	Romans 8:7	74
John 14:5	34	Romans 8:31	16
John 14:8	34	Romans 10:4	69
John 14:22	34	Romans 10:4	80
John 14:15	7	Romans 11	23
John 15:10-11	7	Romans 11:16-24	80
John 19:19	77	Romans 11:18-21	78
John 19:20-21	78	Romans 11:23-24	78
Acts 2	40	1 Corinth. 5:7-8	11
Acts 2	42	1 Corinth. 5:7-8	27
Acts 2:1	40	1 Corinth. 5:7-8	39
Acts 2:2, 6	41	1 Corinth. 10:19	85
Acts 2:6	41	1 Corinth. 10:20	85

General Index

Adam: knew principles of God's law, 2-4; sin of, resulted in carnal nature, 70;

Abel: obeyed and was accepted 2;

Abraham: obeyed God's law, 1, 55, 80; true children of, follow his example, 79, 80;

Abram: saw God the Son, 5;

Adversary: Satan is our adversary, 16;

Against us: 8, 15, 54, 67;

Ahab the king: apostasy of, 84-85, 91; and Elijah, 86-87; (see also "Jezebel")

Alexandria (Egypt), church of: became administrative head of church in North Africa, 44;

Angel in wilderness: carried name of God, 6;

Anicetus: first century Bishop of Rome, 45-46;

Antioch, church of: administrative head of Asian (middle eastern) churches, 44;

Ark of the Covenant: 56;

Antioch: early role, 17; and circumcision, 18;

Animal sacrifices – See "Sacrifices"

Antitypes and types: "met" at the death of Christ, 24, 57; were "matched pairs," 21, 25, 57;

Apostasy: in Israel, 32, 83-86, 91; Christian, 2nd to 4th centuries, 80-81; modern, 86;

Apostles: see Disciples

Ashtoreth: fertility goddess, 84; equivalent names, 85

Atonement, Day of: taught by Paul, 39;

Baptism: death and burial of our "old man of sin," 71;

Barnabas and Paul, first missionary journey, 17;

Beggarly elements (Galatians 4:9): reference to paganism, 75;

Believers in Christ: see Jewish believers; Gentile believers

Bible: see Scripture (Word of God)

Book of the Law (*Torah*): backdrop for Christ's teachings and practices, 56; Christ is true author, 7;

The Elijah Message

72, 73; given to uncircumcised as well as circum-
cised, 18; impresses truth upon our minds, 86; on
Pentecost, accompanied by loud noise, 41;
Irenaeus: Christian leader in second century AD, 45;
Ishtar: Babylonian Queen of Heaven, the goddess of
fertility - same as Astarte, Venus, Diana, Easter, 51;
Israelites: were Christians when obeying God's law, 6;
Jacob: promised to pay 10% of holdings to God, 55;
saw God the Son 5;
James: chaired Jerusalem Council, 18;
Jehovah: is God the Son, 6;
Jeroboam: cast aside divine institutions, 84, 97;
defiant against God, 83-84; established a variant
festival calendar, 83; first king of Northern Israel, 83;
God rebuked, 83-84; schemed to keep people away
from Jerusalem at annual festivals, 83; set up golden
calf idols at Dan and Bethel, 83; worshiped demons,
83;
Jerusalem Council c. 48 AD: 17-22; decision upheld by
Paul, 24; did not end annual festivals, 27; did not
"throw out" the Law of Moses, 19; established
Fellowship Requirements, 19, 22; feasts not discussed
by, 21; held at time of "approaching festivals," 21;
understanding of, 24;
Jesus Christ: Author of Leviticus, 6; Author of statutes
and judgments, 81; believers in, are adopted into
Abraham's family and olive tree, 78; born in autumn,
52; blood of, provides justification, 16; cruel
treatment of, insulting, inspired by Satan, 68; death
of, shows immutability of God's law, 69; died in the
sinner's place, 65, 67, 69; did not abolish God's law,
69, 80; did not sin, 66; embodied God's law (kept
God's law perfectly in human flesh), 56, 66, 69, 80;
gift of, (Holy Spirit) empowers sanctification, 16;
gives (imputes and imparts) His own righteousness to
repentant sinners as a gift, 73; gives us eternal life as
a gift, 9, 71; is God the Son, 6; is the only, loving
and powerful Savior, 6, 65, 67, 73; is the substance
the shadows point to, 15; is the True Jew, 23, 76-77,

80, 81; Jehovah, 6; King of the Jews, 77, 78; Law Giver, 6; life was consistent with the Law He gave to Moses, 56; Lion and the Lamb (Rev. 5:5), 76-77; love for us, inspires our obedience, 68; now sits at the right-hand of the throne of God, 38; obeyed God's law perfectly, 66; observed Passover away from Jerusalem, 21, 39; on the cross, experienced complete separation from God, 65; on the cross, paid the ransom price for sins of mankind, 10, 66, 67; on the cross, sign over His head, 77; on the cross, victorious over Satan, 16, 68; originator of the religion of the Jews, 78; proclaimed freedom of individual conscience; 79; provides only means of salvation, 65; religion of, given to Moses for Israel, 78; resurrection of, is the Firstfruits, 38; retained divine life within Himself, 65; sacrificed as the true Passover Lamb, 38; sacrifice of, procured blessings of the New Covenant for us, 38; said John the Baptist was a manifestation of the promised Elijah, 89; shed blood of, ratified the Everlasting Covenant, 38; showed God's love for mankind, 65, 68; sins of the world (guilt) placed upon Him, 66-67; spoke face to face with Moses, 6; spoke the law (*Torah*) to Moses, 56; source of righteousness for all branches (Jew and Gentile) on olive tree of Israel, 80; suffered in Garden of Gethsemane, 66-67; suffering of, 67; taught His disciples to abide in His Word, 79; truth of, came from His Father, 79; takes away Satan's power to accuse us, 67; taught that God's law is broader than only the Ten Commandments, 55;

Jesus Christ: anticipated the keeping of Passover into the kingdom of God, 38; commanded the keeping of the Feasts of the Lord, 49; did not abolish the feasts, 40; faith of, will be held by end-time believers, 7; is the Firstfruits of the resurrection, 38; is the true Passover Lamb, 38; kept His father's commandments, 7; not in conflict with obedience to God's law, 75; promises love and joy when we keep His commandments, 7; religion available world-wide, 21;

61; given to increase religious instruction, 62; given
to promote holy living, 61; not shadowy types to end
at the death of Christ, 61; reviewed obligation to
keep the seventh-day Sabbath, 60; specify man's
duty to man, 62; shut out pagan practices, 61; (see
"Judgments and Statutes")
Judgments and Statutes: are the "fine print" of the
Moral Law, 19, 57-58, 60-62; are to be cherished,
63; authored by Jesus Christ, 63, 81; connect to the
Ten Commandments, 54, 57, 63-64; define and
explain the Moral Law, 62; disobedience to, is
opposition to Christ, 81; part of the Everlasting/New
Covenant, 54, 64; never to lose their force, 61, 63,
64; spoken by God the Son directly to Moses, 57, 81;
to be proclaimed by God's holy people in the end
time, 64; (see also, Statutes and Judgments)
Justification: gift of God's grace, 72; pardon for our
sins, 72; sets us in right relationship to God's law, 72;
through cleansing power of Christ's blood, 72;
Kingdom of Heaven: only those will enter, who are
obedient to God's commandments, 81;
Law: word in New Testament: comes from Greek word
nomos, a general word for law: civil law, religious
law, natural law or "ultimate truth principle," 70;
Law: word in Old Testament: comes from Hebrew word
"Torah" – see "Book of the Law"
Law Giver of Old Testament is God the Son, 6;
Law of Carnality: 71; carnal mind is enmity against
God and His law, 73; sinful heart, only changed by
power of Christ through the Holy Spirit, 74;
Law of God (Moral Law), broader than Ten Commandments, 55; cannot be changed, 69; codified in writing
at Mt. Sinai, 1, 55; commandments of, are holy, just
and good, 8; demands perfect obedience for
salvation, 73; established (met) by gift of grace,
through faith, 69; foundational principles of, 3, 74;
foundation of God's government, 69; God's
explanation of love, 68, 74, 74, 81; impossible for
sinful humans to keep without God's help and power,

The Elijah Message

those who choose it are doomed to disobey God, 30;

Old Testament, God of: is God of love, 5;

Old Testament, religion of: not to be superseded by the New Testament, 81; is further advanced and unfolded in the New Testament, 81 (see "Religion of the Bible")

Olive tree: symbol of (spiritual) Israel, 78;

Omer: 50-day count from Early Firstfruits to Pentecost, 37;

Paganism: not to be mixed with God's religion, 61, 75;

Passover: Christ is the true Passover Lamb, 38; day of Christ's crucifixion, 35; and new-moon calendar, 35-36; observed by Jesus Christ at Capernaum, 21;

Passover, Messianic: memorial of Christ's sacrifice, 34-35, 43, 46; called *Pascha* in Greek New Testament, 13, 14; Christ connected the Lord's Supper with the Passover, 35; complete fulfillment of, awaits the kingdom of God, 38; Cup after Supper, 33; elements of, teach about Christ's plan of salvation, 46; held at time appointed, 34; kept by apostles and Christians to the end of first century AD and beyond, 46-48; kept by Paul with Gentile believers at Philippi, 26-27; Lord's Supper of the Gospels, 27, 34, 46; not part of the ceremonial law, 12; Paul commanded Corinthian believers to keep, 27; portrays the terms of the New Covenant, 38; prophetic reminder of final deliverance from sin, 43; reminds us of Jesus' sacrifice to deliver us from the Egypt of sin, 38, 43;

Passover *Seder*: first century AD/CE, 33; elements of, seen in Christ's Lord's Supper, 34, 35; four cups based on God's "I will" promises in Exodus, 34; Jesus infused Messianic meaning into elements of, 34-35; elements of, commanded in Exodus, 34;

Paul and Barnabas: first missionary journey, 17; and circumcision controversy, 18;

Paul: and God's traditions, 11; did not object to circumcision for Jews, 23; did not observe the ceremonial law after his conversion, 26; had Timothy circumcised after the Jerusalem Council, 23; honored the decision of the Jerusalem Council (48 AD) regarding Gentiles, 24; kept the feasts as a Christian, 11, 12, 26, 39; memorized the *Torah*, 15; observed Passover with the Philippian (Gentile) believers, 12, 26; observed Pentecost, 11, 26, 39; observed the Lord's religious calendar taught in the Torah, 26, 39; observed Unleavened Bread, 11, 26, 39; preached that rites of ceremonial law had ended, 12, 20, 26; taught that worshiping idols is connected to demon worship, 85; taught types and antitypes in Hebrews, 21; taught his Gentile converts to keep the annual festivals, 14, 26-27, 39; warns Christians to stay away from demon worship, 85; was a Jew, 12, 26;

Paul and Peter: 17;

Penalty: for breaking God's law, 9;

Pentecost: day on which Christ anointed His disciples with the Holy Spirit, 42; celebrated giving of the Law, and establishment of Israel as a nation, 42; did not end at the cross, 42; Feast of the Lord observed annually, 13; Greek word, meaning "50 days," 42; Jewish leaders at temple, mocked disciples on, 42; New Testament Greek name for *Shavuot* or Feast of Weeks, 14; observed by disciples at the Temple, after Christ's ascension, 41; observed by Paul as a Christian, 11; outpouring of Holy Spirit upon, 18; people crowded into the temple on, 42;

Peter: and Cornelius, 17; and Gentile converts, 17-18;

Peter and Paul: 17;

Pharisees: claimed Abraham as their father, 79;

Philippian Christians: taught by Paul to keep the Messianic Passover, 26-27; were primarily Gentile believers, 26;

Polycarp: Christian pastor at Smyrna in second century AD, 45; conflict with Bishop of Rome (Easter vs Passover), 45; Gentile Christian, disciple of John the Apostle, 45; observed Passover with John and the other Apostles, 46; martyred on Passover, 46;

Polycrates: Bishop of church at Ephesus, 47; controversy with Bishop of Rome over Passover vs Easter, 47; disciple of Polycarp, 46; Gentile Christian

definitely arranged and expressed, 3; principles the same as before fall, 2; additional (particular) precepts given after fall, 2;

Theophanies: God seen by humans was always God the Son, 5, 6;

Theophanies: God seen by Abram, 5; by Hagar, 5; by Jacob, 5; by Moses, 6;

Throne of God: connected to His law, 4;

Throne of God: foundation of, is righteousness and justice, 5; law is foundation of, 5;

Tithe: Abraham paid tithe to Melchizedek, 55; commanded to be eaten at Feasts in Jerusalem, 55; available equally to all Levites, 59; Jacob's promise to tithe, 55; Levites paid heave offering to the central sanctuary, 59; Levites supported by tithe of the third year, 58-59; not discussed by Jerusalem Council (48 AD), 22; widows and orphans to share in tithe of the third year, 58;

Torah (written): blessings of obedience to, 4; fence that protects, 4; includes statutes and judgments, 4; not nullified by Jerusalem Council, 19; preached weekly in synagogue, 20, 22; teaches the Lord's religious calendar, 26;

Traditions, God's: 11;

Traditions of men: 11;

Trespasses: of the Law, brings death 8; in Colossians, 9-10;

Tree of Life: and commandment keepers, 4;

Truth: Jesus' truth came from His Father, 79; knowing the truth (of God's Word) brings freedom, 79;

Types and Antitypes: were "matched pairs," 21, 25, 57; types ended when replaced by "something better" 57; (see "Antitypes and Types")

Types: ended at the cross, 21, 25; pointed to the Antitypes, 25; "place-holders" that were ended by their "better" antitypes, 21, 25, 57;

Uncircumcised: Gentiles, 8; believers at Colossae, 8; in the 15th chapter of Acts, 17; Jews saw no salvation hope for, 18; not to be basis for discrimination among

Ruach Eloi

Ru-ach El-oi fall on me! Ru-ach El-oi strength-en me!

Speak the word, Lord; touch my heart, Lord; May I lis-ten, Lord, to Thee.

May I wor-ship only Thee – to no o-ther bend the knee.

Your Mess-i-ah send to me: Ye-shu-a ben Da-vid.